There are some Cases so singularly reasonabl
considered, the more Weight th

Thomas Paine 1772

The Thomas Paine Society UK

Paul Myles, 13 Hill Road, Lewes, East Sussex, BN7 1DB

www.thomaspaineuk.com

Ordering Information: by post 13 Hill Road Lewes East Sussex pmyles.pm@gmail.com

Quantity sales. Special discounts are available on quantity purchases by corporations, associations, and others. For details, contact the "Special Sales Department" at the address above.

The Rise of Thomas Paine and The Case of the Officers of Excise by Paul Myles. 1st edition. ISBN 978-1-9993263-0-2

ILLUSTRATION BY PENELOPE PARKER AFTER THE PORTRAIT OF THOMAS PAINE IN LONDON 1790
(Artist Unknown)

To my wife Kathy for her lifelong support and encouragement

Rise of Thomas Paine and The Case of The Officers of Excise

THE FIRST NATIONAL ORGANISATION OF WORKERS IN THE
UNITED KINGDOM FOR BETTER PAY AND CONDITIONS

Paul Myles

The Thomas Paine Society UK

Lewes England

Chapters

Appendices

CHAPTER 1

Introduction

Thomas Paine wrote *The Case of the Officers of Excise* in support of a petition for higher pay. In Paine's own words, '**A Petition for this purpose has been circulated thro' every part of the Kingdom, and signed by all the officers therein.**' The problem was that the 3,000 signatures were missing. Some of these recently came to light, found in the vaults of the National Archive, tucked away, not classified, in one of the Treasury Boxes. At first these just looked like an earlier attempt from some isolated Excise Officers, but further findings revealed what we now know to be a long, slow-burning campaign culminating in Thomas Paine's authorship of *The Case of The Officers of Excise*. This was the result of a meeting of two men: George Lewis Scott, a commissioner working at the highest level, and Thomas Paine, an outrider working at the lowest level. The anxiety of a nation was crystallised in this pamphlet, which exposed the underbelly of corruption. This corruption was borne by low pay at one end and greed at the other, and contributed to the national anxiety regarding insufficient revenue for both the Crown and efficient government.

Matters of national importance came to a head during Thomas Paine's time in Lewes (1768-1774). George III had changed the political landscape from Whig to Tory in the years since he was crowned in 1760. The newspapers were aflame with reports of ministerial mismanagement. The Excise Service was near to collapse due to long-term corruption. The King was under pressure due to his poor financial settlement from the Civil List. The Excise Revenue was the main collection agency for those very funds. The Revenue was under pressure due to widespread corruption. *The Case* and the petition was the solution. But would anybody listen?

The pamphlet that Paine wrote in Lewes, *The Case of The Officers of Excise*, can be recognised as the culmination of the first national organisation of workers appealing for better working conditions and fair pay. This was the first organised effort on a national scale from within the government by employees, a foreshadowing of later trade unions. This is a new story about Paine during this period. He is popularly known as an anti-monarchist, republican and critic of organised religion, and rightly so since these views are clearly laid out in his later writing, but he was not so in Lewes from 1768-1774. The content of *The Case of The Officers of Excise* showed that he was in support of his King at the time. The thrust of *The Case* was how to improve the Excise Service, and at the same time help his king and country.

This investigation will use contemporary records that relate to Paine's experience in the Excise Service. The campaign that was mounted for better pay and conditions will show what life was like for officers and their families. New findings have been found in the National Archives, showing signatures that until now were considered missing from that campaign. The crisis of corruption in the Excise Service in Cornwall will be shown to be a turning point, prompting action to stem the nationwide fraud in the Excise. Minute book entries pertaining to Paine will be laid out in chronological order completely for the first time. Other original sources will include entries from the first biographer of Paine, George Chalmers, and letters from Paine at the time to the Excise Office as well as later ones referring to his relationship with George Lewis Scott, the senior Commissioner of the Board of Excise. Additionally, Benjamin Franklin's letter recommending Paine to his son-in-law in America will be shown alongside other letters from Franklin written at the same time. These foreshadowed the War of Independence between Britain and the North American colonies.

Articles in *The Sussex Weekly Advertiser or Lewes Journal*, recently digitised, will reveal a nation in unrest whilst Paine was in Lewes. Storylines from the newspaper will be tracked through the months to show the cacophony of complaint about the King and his Ministry. The storylines were written in a way that amplified the arguments, providing the perfect foil to what Paine experienced working inside the largest government organ. It will be argued here that reading these articles further shaped Paine's political thought at the same time as he was developing his writing skills. Many biographies have described what might have influenced Paine: Quakerism, Methodism, and even just living in the towns of Thetford and Lewes. These arguments will not be dismissed, but will not be repeated in depth here. This is an attempt to understand what Paine experienced and what may have influenced his thinking. It will be argued that he developed, along with others, a sense that the government in England was utterly out of touch to the point of bungling. It was this conviction that eventually led Paine to leave England's shores for America.

These details help explain how Thomas Paine rapidly ascended from the lowly position of an outrider of Excise in Lewes in 1768 to a writer of world-changing influence in America in 1776. His first widely published pamphlet in America, *Common Sense*, kindled the American War of Independence. This was closely followed by thirteen *Crisis Papers*, which steadied the American troops during the War of Independence, in which Paine named, for the first time, The United States of America.

Paine suffered a mixed reception as soon as he moved into to the public sphere with *Common Sense*. He had opponents from the outset of his public writing career. America was divided about whether to break free from Great Britain. He inevitably drew detractors from the Tories in the North American colonies and of course from many back in England. George Chalmers was Paine's first biographer, writing in 1791. He witnessed at first hand the trouble caused by the North American colonists who objected to what they saw as unfair taxation and treatment by King George III and his ministers. Before Paine arrived in America, Chalmers had suffered financial loss as a result of the early North American insurgence, and as a result was primed to write a denigration of Paine's character later on, after Paine's *Rights of Man* was published in England. It was from this first biography, *The Life of Thomas Pain; The Author of Rights of Man with a Defence of His Writings,*[1] that the well of negative attacks on Thomas Paine started, and the well has never quite dried up. Chalmers wrote under the pseudonym of Francis Oldys and was commissioned by a government terrified that the French Revolution might spread to the United Kingdom. The British establishment viewed *Rights of Man* as dangerous; it was cited in France, and Paine had already kindled the American War of Independence with *Common Sense* some twenty years earlier.

Chalmers was an exacting and assiduous researcher. Although he never missed an opportunity to make Paine out to be a villain, official records were made available to him, and in most cases his account is accurate. We will turn to him from time to time. Where he allowed Paine some latitude, it is because he really had to. His rare acknowledgement of Paine's nascent honesty and ability will be referred to as this story unfolds.

Paine is recognised as a very powerful writer, often quoted by presidents of the United States of America, most recently by Barack Obama in both his inaugural speeches. Prolific, his writing spanned continents during one of the most cataclysmic periods of change across the Atlantic Seaboard in Great Britain, France, and America. Paine walked with the giants of his time; a founding father of The United States of America, he was invited onto the French Assembly soon after the revolution. He was influential in the birth of two new republican states.

Rights of Man replied to critics of the French Revolution and laid out the blueprint for a social state that looked after all members of society. Paine addressed organised religion in his *Age of Reason,* reserving his most vitriolic comments for Christians, whilst confirming his position as a deist. Philip Fon-

---

[1] Francis Oldys [George Chalmers], *The Life of Thomas Pain; The Author of Rights of Man with a Defence of His Writings* (3rd Edition, London, 1791).

er provided the most comprehensive collection of Paine's writing in two volumes including dissertations, songs, poems, correspondence and memorials. Eric Foner wrote authoritatively on Paine, as did Greg Claeys, Bruce Kuklick, and many other of the finest academics in the discipline. Bill Speck authored *A Political Biography of Thomas Paine* in 2013, bringing the research up to date at that time.

Paine has been a signal voice over the years. Due to the sparse detail available about his early life, there has been much speculation over what influences might have shaped his convictions. His father was a Quaker, his mother an Anglican. There is some evidence that he was helped by, and followed, the Methodist faith in the time before he joined the Excise Service. There are very few references to his own early life from his own pen. This story will look closely at the way his thought might have developed from his experience in the Excise Service and his time in Lewes, as well as the associations he made with influential people as a result of those two factors.

George Hindmarch was a member of The Thomas Paine Society UK and held a long fascination with Paine. An Excise Officer himself, George knew how to interpret the *Excise Minute Book,* the daily entries made about all officer appointments, movements, and discipline, which was read out to the Commissioners in order for them to manage the national workforce. In his small book, *Thomas Paine: The Case of the King of England and his Officers of Excise,* he explained how the concise record-keeping of the 18c Excise Service kept track of the movement of officers, as well as their recruitment and dismissals, with meticulous accounts.

Hindmarch named George Lewis Scott as the man who plucked Paine from obscurity. Scott was an establishment man, previously a tutor to King George III during the latter's minority. That this gifted mathematician who was intimate with the royal family masterminded an appeal from the lowly workforce seemed unlikely, but Hindmarch's forensic trawl proved it to be the case. Hindmarch wrote several articles on Paine. His writing did not use references, but fortunately the time spent verifying his sources led to the discovery of additional useful documents, including some that seemed to indicate earlier attempts by the Excise Officers of Wales and Hereford to claim higher pay. This finding prompted a deeper look into the extraordinary minute entries about the collapse of the Excise Collection in Cornwall at the same time.

The Case of The Officers of Excise was written in 1772 in Lewes. Until Hindmarch wrote in 1998, most biographers followed the first damning biography of Paine written by George Chalmers in citing Paine as a kind of rabble-rouser who wrote *The Case* at the behest of his fellow lowly officers. What they did not have access to was Paine's private letter to Oliver Goldsmith from the time *The Case* was written, wherein he enclosed a copy of *The Case* and wrote, '*I should not have undertaken it, had I not been particularly applied to by some of my superiors in office.'*[2] The reality of a diligent civil servant working for his superiors is contrary to many accounts, which portray Paine as a troublemaker and rebel. The information revealed in this account allows us to reconsider Paine's development in Lewes. An analysis of *The Case* reveals for the first time some personal details of Paine's life from his experience in the Excise.

The town of Lewes had a part to play in Paine's development. Colin Brent wrote the best explanation of this in 'Thirty Something', a reference to Paine's age during his time in Lewes, laying out the reasons why this was so. Lewes was an open society, not a rotten borough, and elections were hotly contested. It had a simple form of local government, a Court Leet, which Paine sat on. The way the town was run meant one did not have to be a freeman of the town to do business. Rather, anyone could, and Paine himself did so later on as a tobacconist. Paine attended the vestry meetings that administered the Poor Law. He moved in with Samuel Ollive in Bull House on arrival in Lewes. Ollive was the High Constable that year, the returning officer in an election year. The election was so hotly contested that he abstained from voting for himself. The Duke of Newcastle, a political mastermind, owned a house close to Lewes, in Laughton, and visited when needed to dispense favours in order to get his two parliamentary candidates elected. Newcastle was the First Lord of the Treasury when Scott was appointed as a Commissioner of Excise in 1758. Newcastle died in 1768, the year Paine rode into Lewes, after having been deserted by previous electioneering allies in Lewes. Newcastle had failed to get his preferred candidates elected this time after many years of secure support. Lewes was a dissenting town with a mix of Independents, Presbyterians, Quakers, and Baptists, and also a Whig town that supported John Wilkes in opposition to the Crown and Ministry.[3]

William Lee was the owner, editor and printer of the first weekly newspaper in Sussex, based in Lewes: *The Sussex Weekly Advertiser or Lewes Journal*. This was established in 1746. By the time Thomas Paine came to town in 1768 it was a firmly established and lively newspaper. Lee was apprenticed in London under James Bettenham as a stationer; the Stationers' guild was one of the oldest in London and a central component of the 18c printing world. Lee printed four thousand copies of *The Case* for Paine in Lewes under the instruction of Scott. It will be considered that Lee was an important individual in realising Paine's nascent ability to write clearly. Paine's letters were printed in the newspaper. Given this close association with the owner of the newspa-

---

[2] Thomas Paine, 'Letter to Oliver Goldsmith', 21 December 1772, *The Complete Writings of Thomas Paine*, ed. Philip S. Foner, vol. 2 (New York, 1945), p. 1129.

[3] Colin Brent, 'Thirty Something: Thomas Paine at Bull House in Lewes, 1768-74 - Six Formative Years', *Sussex Archaeological Society Collections*, vol. 147 (2009), pp. 153-67.

per, it can be safely assumed that Paine would have been a regular reader as well as a contributor.

To conclude this introduction, I would like to make it clear that this account is not a biography of Paine. Whilst there are some biographical details, this is an attempt to adopt a forensic approach to investigate matters that would have impressed directly on Paine's consciousness. The minute book entries regarding Paine in the Excise Service will be shown in a timeline for the first time, with additional supporting evidence from recent research. Furthermore, *The Case* will be analysed in more detail than before. The local newspaper, now digitised in PDF form, will be shown as an important contributor to Paine's political development during his time in Lewes. This account will move us closer to the way this enigmatic Englishman formed his philosophical and political viewpoints in America, France and England, which resound to this day.

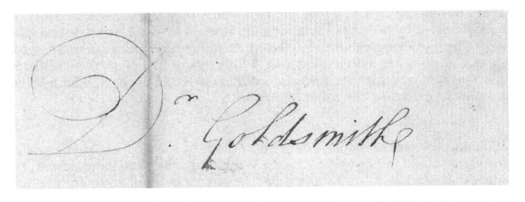

LETTER TO OLIVER GOLDSMITH FROM THOMAS PAINE DEC 21 1772

Honoured Sir

  Herewith I present you with a Case of the Officers of Excise. A Compliment of this kind from an entire Stranger may appear somewhat singular; But the following reasons and Informations, will I presume sufficiently apologise.

  I act myself in the humble Station of an Officer of Excise tho' somewhat differently circumstanced to what many of them are, and have been the Principal Promoter of a Plan for applying to Parliament this Session for an encrease of Salary. A Petition for this Purpose has been circulated thro' every Part of the Kingdom, and Signed by all the officers therein. A Subscription of three shillings P.r Officer is raised, amounting to upwards of five hundred pounds for supporting the Expences.

  The Excise Officers in all Cities and Corporate Towns have obtained Letters of Recommendation from the Electors to the Members in their behalf, many or most of whom have Promised their Support. The enclosed Case we have presented to most of the Members and shall to all before the Petition appears in the House.—

  The Memorial before you met with so much approbation while in Manuscript, that I was advised to print four Thousand Copies. Three Thousand of which were Subscribed for by the Officers in general, and the remaining 1000 reserved for presents.

  Since the delivering them, I have received so many Letters of Thanks and approbation for the Performance that were I not rather singularly Modest, I should insensibly become a little Vain.

  The Literary Fame of D.r Goldsmith has induced me

LETTER TO OLIVER GOLDSMITH DEC 21 1772

to present one to him. Such as it is, 'tis my first and only attempt. and even now I should not have undertaken it had I not been particularly applied to. by some of my Superiors in office..

I have some few Questions to Trouble D. Goldsmith with and should esteem his company for an hour or two, to partake of a Bottle of Wine or any thing else, and apologise for this trouble, as a singular favour confered on

His unknown
Humble Ser.
and admirer

Excise Coffee House &
Broad Street

Dec. 21. 72[?]

Tho: Pain

P. S. shall take the Liberty of waiting on you in a day or two

LETTER TO OLIVER GOLDSMITH DEC 21 1772

CHAPTER 2

George Hindmarch showed the way

Early Biographies

The first biography of Paine was written by George Chalmers, a government-paid assassin of Paine's character. Chalmers's account was accurate but twisted to defame. Though written in devotion, the biography by Clio Rickman, Paine's friend in life, lacked real detail. Many biographies have followed, almost perennially, most of them in defence of Paine against Chalmers or James Cheetham, another early sharp critic of Paine, but most of these lack any real or new detail of Paine's life in England up to the age of 37, when he left Lewes and arrived in North America for the first time.

George Hindmarch, a retired Officer of Excise with a lifelong fascination with Thomas Paine, showed the way. Through his occupation and interest he developed an ability to interpret the 18c *Excise Board and Secretariat: Minute Books* and other official records surround the service, and a great deal of information became available to him by examining specialised archival records. With these records, Hindmarch revealed the details of everyday movements, dismissals, and appointments of officers throughout all levels of the service: small details that add up to an explanation. He took a bottom-up approach to assess the reasons behind actions, the financial imperatives that were operating right through the government machine.

The finding of George Hindmarch's book, *Thomas Paine: The Case of the King of England and His Officers of Excise*, published in 1998,[4] was a breakthrough moment. Initially it was not available other than in the British Library. Difficult to read and written without references, it was a while before I decided it was worth following up the leads and assertions that were made within. After enquiries were made to The Thomas Paine Society UK, copies of the book were made available by Robert Morell, editor of the Society's journal. Inside the front cover, it states: *'Published Privately 1998 and available only from the author.'* All copies of the book were sent to the Society after George Hind-

---

[4] George Hindmarch, *Thomas Paine: The Case of the King of England and his Officers of Excise* (published privately, 1998).

march died. Subsequently his widow made available his remaining manuscripts and what research material remained on the condition that they were lodged with the East Sussex Records Office, The Keep, where they now reside. Graham Smith, the librarian and archivist for the Customs and Excise, published *Something to Declare* in 1980. This publication along with the information from Hindmarch has provided a portal into the secretive world of 18c Excise collection.

Up until Hindmarch's book, most biographers had written that Paine acted as a rebel for his fellow Excise men in a claim for higher wages during the Lewes period; when this came to the notice of his superiors in the Excise, they discharged him from the service in disgrace. Hindmarch has forensically proved that this was far from the truth. In fact, Paine was selected out of 3,000 Officers of Excise *by his superiors* to pen the pamphlet. It has been popular to frame Paine as an anti-royal activist in Lewes. Most biographers had fallen into this trap, but Hindmarch showed us that, contrary to this assertion, Paine was a loyal subject of King George III in his position as a civil servant. Paine, rather than acting as an insurgent, wrote *The Case of The Officers of Excise* under the instruction of George Lewis Scott, a Commissioner of Excise. Scott had previously been preceptor to King George III in his minority, and had direct access to the inner workings of the royal family over two generations.

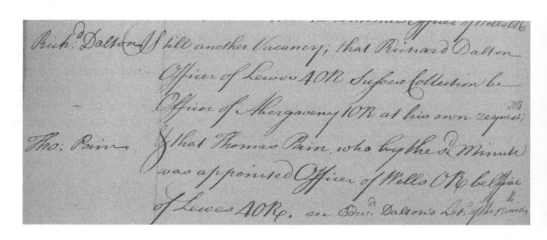

EXCISE MINUTE BOOK: THOMAS PAIN BE OFFICER OF LEWES 4TH OUT RIDE 1768

CHAPTER 3

History of the Excise Service

The Excise Service was separate from the Customs Service and followed a different path of development, with both combining only in 1909. The Customs Service, dealing with import duties, had an old lineage and can be traced back to Anglo Saxon times. The Excise was started during the Civil War in England as a means of money-raising for the Parliamentary force in 1643. It continued after the restoration, being farmed out to wealthy merchants and gentlemen who purchased the right to collect taxes for the Crown, earning 6% of the sums collected. Already an efficient organisation, the collection was brought into central control by the establishment of a Board of Commissioners of Excise to administer the service in 1683. Excise was a duty levied on home-produced goods such as beer, ale, spirits, cider, and soap. The goods liable to duty grew each year and included a range of imported goods. Later the list grew to include meat, salt, clothes, hats, paper, starch, glass, hops, leather, linen, tobacco, fish, and oils. The many existing Excise Officers nationwide were added to with some new posts, creating a national civil service in the direct employment of the monarch. The pay of civil servants was set by the Lords of the Treasury, and the money came from the budget allocated to the king by Parliament, the Civil List.

A tension had developed between the king and Parliament. The tripartite agreement made after the Glorious Revolution of 1688 divided power between the monarch, the House of Lords, and the House of Commons. The first monarch of this new system, William III, had no guaranteed income and nearly returned to his original home, Holland. Although he was granted supremacy in the new balance of power, the monarch was really the weakest of the three components, as sufficient finances for the Crown had not been allocated. Eventually, not wanting to be exposed to attack by the deposed Stuarts, who had French backing, the Civil List was created by a parliamentary act in 1698. Parliament assumed responsibility for all national debts and the armed forces; the Crown was made responsible for the civil expenses of government.

The way that the Civil List was conceived, and the way that it developed from its beginnings through to King George III, was of particular interest to George Hindmarch. He focused on the structure and weaknesses of the Civil List from an Excise Officer's point of view, in other words from within the system. This was an unusual perspective. Most history is written by historians, and most of these historians are professional, often from within academic institutions. Hindmarch sharply pointed this out to his readers, castigating the profession of history in the process. He informed us that history-writing about Thomas Paine had been lazy, subject to fashion and the political persuasion of the day. He had a point. Most later biographers had copied the early biographers with perhaps a sprinkling of new observation, but their writings had not been based on rigorous research.

Parliament had control over the amount that was paid to the monarch. Excise receipts went to the Treasury. The amount granted to the monarch through the Civil List was tightly controlled by Parliament, especially throughout the reign of George III. The Civil List payments were under even more scrutiny in the period leading up to 1771, when Paine was recruited to write *The Case of The Officers of Excise*. It can be seen from the articles in *The Sussex Weekly Advertiser or Lewes Journal* that the country was aflame with criticism of the monarch and his corrupt ministry. This will be addressed later, in a chapter detailing Paine's relationship with the owner of the newspaper, William Lee, and the reporting style that Lee adopted.

Hindmarch tracked the amounts that were paid to successive monarchs. In 1698, £700,000 was paid to the first to receive it, William III, after some wrangling to get any payment at all. By 1712, Queen Anne had incurred debts of £500,000 which, after being settled by central arrangements, incited a contest between Crown and Parliament over the appropriate sum to be granted to the Crown in the Civil List. There was a new negotiation on every succession. George I, the first of the Hanoverian kings, often maligned for his lack of fluent English, was astute in a fiscal sense. He negotiated through an intermediary, a chief minister, eventually choosing Robert Walpole, who effectively became the first Prime Minister. Though this adroit approach, the first Hanoverian monarch secured £700,000 a year and also a further £100,000 for his heir, the future George II.

Walpole negotiated again in 1727 on behalf of King George II, who was granted the most generous initial Civil List of any Hanoverian King, the sum of £800,000. This was further enhanced by the assurance that any shortfall, if expenditure was larger than the list, would automatically be made up for by Parliament. However, if there were any excess, the King could keep it. In addition to this there was made provision that the royal income could grow with the increasing national income, with the result that by the end of his reign the payment had grown by 10% to £876,988. Hindmarch calculated that had this arrangement had been continued for his grandson, George III, by 1777 the Civil List would have reached £1,000,000, but this was not to be.

Whilst Walpole had eased the transition of power and income between the first two Hanoverian kings, he had passed away by the time the young George III came to the throne in 1760. His negotiations with Parliament were not as shrewd as Walpole's. Most income came from Excise duties, with very little coming from the Crown estates, which he surrendered in return for a Civil List annuity, but this time without the guaranteed rise to match any higher income that might come about from an increasing economy or inflation. Therefore, the Civil List was fixed at £800,000. Debts were run up in addition to the Civil List, which Parliament had to settle from time to time. There was tangible political change after the accession of George III; he favoured Tory ministers over the Whig incumbents. Whigs had been accustomed to the ascendency and in response mounted fierce political battles against the new Tory ministers.

There was some room for manoeuvring by the Crown from within the Civil List. Part of the expenditure from the Civil List was pre-arranged and carried forward from the previous reign, under the Treasury's supervision. The major income came from the two separate entities of Customs and Excise. These two organisations were under the control of separate boards, each responsible to the Treasury, which kept a watchful eye on their respective accounting practices. There were two special channels of Civil List expenditure by the monarch from which Treasury scrutiny was denied. The first was the Privy Purse, from which the king paid his personal and household expenses. The second was the king's outlay on Secret Services, which included diplomatic services. The need for absolute secrecy placed the details of payments beyond the reach of parliamentary challenge. Some of the Secret Service payments were pensions granted to individuals for various reasons. These payments often reached public knowledge as those who received them often let it slip out.

The opposition in the Commons, bolstered by the Whig faction, suspected that bribes were issued from the Civil List, via Secret Service payments, in order to obtain support for Ministers in royal favour. In other words, that covert pensions were paid in order to keep the opposition out. One recipient, Samuel Johnson, made this public, openly stating that as a former Jacobite upholding the Stuart values of the divine right of kings:

> 'It is true that I cannot now curse the House of Hanover; nor would it be decent for me to drink King James's health in the wine that King George gives me money to pay for. But, Sir, I think that the pleasure of cursing the House of Hanover, and drinking King James's health, are amply overbalanced by three hundred pounds a year.'[5]

---

[5] James Boswell, *The Life of Samuel Johnson*, vol. 1 (New York, 1835), p. 195.

CHAPTER 4

Paine's progress through the Excise Service

Hindmarch turned to examine Thomas Paine's progress through the Excise Service. This part of the story was produced in a paper entitled 'The First Excise Period,' submitted to The Thomas Paine Society UK and a few other interested parties.[6] To date, these findings have not been published to the public. Hindmarch himself declared that it contained many extracts from official papers and therefore was not suitable for the general reader. Drawing together information from these papers, the story presented in the essay showed a critical component of the making of *The Case*. This was where close attention to the minute book, with a certain knowledge about how the service functioned, paid dividends. A story emerged that was contrary to the popular legend that Paine was a drifter in his early life, constantly failing at whatever he tried. The personal story of Paine from within the Excise shows us how Paine witnessed at first hand how mismanagement at the national level caused corruption among Officers of Excise at all levels, especially those on the front line.

Hindmarch used the Excise *General Letter Books, Minute Books,* and the *Board's Entry Books of Correspondence with the Treasury.* The *Minute Books,* however, are the most complete and revealing source he used. They contain minutes of the meetings of the Board of Commissioners in which the correspondence from the collections were read out to the Commissioners and their responses recorded. These included descriptions of the character traits of Excise Officers.

After the Excise was brought under central control in 1683, a Board of Commissioners was established to oversee the organisation on a day-to-day basis. Under the new board, the service was separated into a Country service and a London service. The Country service was further divided into 39 'Collections', generally following county borders. Wales was divided into four

---

[6] George Hindmarch, 'Thomas Paine: The First Excise Period' (two versions, unpublished, East Sussex Records Offices, The Keep, ACC 10140/2).

ridings: East, West, North and Middle. Each Collection, headed by an officer called a Collector who represented the Commissioners, had a number of districts, each controlled by a Supervisor. By 1770, the number of Collections in the Country service had risen to 53. The officers were mostly centred in market towns, with some of the larger towns having more than one officer. The areas in such towns were called 'divisions,' and the country areas outside the towns were called 'out rides.' The London service was divided into categories: Brewery, Distillery, Tea, Coffee, and Chocolate, amongst others. The total strength of the Excise department in 1771 was over 3,000. There were nine Commissioners, situated in Broad Street in London, with a staff of 230. Country officers numbered 2,736, under 256 Supervisors, who reported to 53 Collectors.[7]

Paine would most likely have learnt about the Excise Service from his father-in-law, James Lambert, whilst in Dover during his brief marriage to Mary Lambert. In particular, he would have learnt about discipline in the service, as James Lambert was discharged from duty in 1735 for a variety of errors at breweries.

The lengthy process of petitioning to be an Officer of Excise belied the struggle to ensure honesty in the service. Layers of verification about suitability, garnished with oaths, revealed a national insecurity. Financial security was a worry, but there was also a fear of the threat from the deposed Stuart dynasty. Therefore, allegiance to the Hanoverian king was reinforced as often as possible; fealty to the House of Hanover and Protestant Christianity was intertwined with a denial of the Catholic faith. The contrast between this process and the reality of the practices in the Excise could not have been greater. Paine's experience after admission was one of corruption and deceit. He was almost immediately caught up in venal practice, in which he would take no part.

The terms of Royal Gauger and Officer of Excise were interchangeable. To be an Officer of Excise required the ability to interpret complicated and exacting rules in order to perform well. The laws, regulations and exemptions were ever changing with different manufacturing processes.

A comprehensive manual, *The Royal Gauger,* was authored by Charles Leadbetter in 1739, running through seven editions up to 1779. It was a huge volume of 450 pages with detailed instructions. At the beginning of this manual he defined what exactly gauging meant: '*the methods of finding the contents of all sorts of Cisterns, Coppers, Backs, Coolers, Tuns, Stills and Casks, when full, or Part empty.*' He showed examples of how to do this using '*The Pen and Sliding Rule,*' and further added, '*and this not in Ale, Beer, Wine and Malt only; but in*

---

[7] George Hindmarch, 'Thomas Paine: The Excise Background', *The Thomas Paine Society Bulletin,* vol. 5, no. 4 (1977), p. 8.

Made-Wines, Soap, Starch, Candles, Hops, Coffee, Tea, Chocolate, all Sorts of Leather, Paper, etc.'[8]

Leadbetter, who was an Officer of Excise before he wrote the manual, but also famous as a mathematician, recorded the rule that someone might become an Officer of Excise in the following manner:

> '*The method of obtaining Employment in the Excise is by petitioning the Commissioners for an Order to be instructed, and in order to that, the Person where he was born a certificate of his Age, which must not be less than 21 or more than 30; and if he is married he must have no more than two children.*'

Any expectant officer could not make the petition himself. Paine's sponsor was Mr. Cocksedge, the Recorder at Thetford, whose assistance was probably sought by Frances, Paine's mother. Her father was a Thetford attorney. In the system of patronage at play, deference to a superior was rewarded by the humble approach of those below them seeking favours. The order of instruction was by the Commissioner Mr. Frankland. Mr. Cocksedge may have personally known Frankland, or perhaps one of the other nine Commissioners. The pleasure of issuing orders allowing one to start the long process of application was shared by the Commissioners on an equal basis, in rotation.

Particular care was taken to establish the applicant's date of birth and the trade he had been apprenticed to. The candidate then had to nominate two guarantors to stand security for his future handling of Excise revenue to the sum of £20, almost half a year's salary for an Officer of Excise. The candidate would have paid 20 shillings to the Supervisor for his certificate and, after acceptance, 40 shillings to the Officer who then instructed him.

There were stringent conditions in place to ensure applicants reached the required standard. Checks were made on health, sobriety, intelligence, and that the applicant possessed a sound understanding of mathematics. Their handwriting had to be proficient, and they had to be free of debts, loyal to the government, and prove membership of the Church of England.

It didn't stop there. According to Leadbetter, after all the above steps were taken, if the petitioner could not obtain the positive countenance of some gentleman, preferably a Member of Parliament, that was personally acquainted with one of the Commissioners to frequently remind the Commissioner of his promise, then the petition would certainly come to nothing. There was so much competition for places that only the most ardent efforts on behalf of an

---

[8] Charles Leadbetter, *The Royal Gauger; Or, Gauging Made Perfectly Easy, as it is Actually Practised by the Officers of His Majesty's Revenue of Excise. In Two Parts.* (London, 1750), frontispiece (title page).

applicant would gain an appointment.[9] Oaths of allegiance and supremacy had to be taken either before two Justices of the Peace or one of the Barons of the Exchequer; these oaths can be seen in Appendix One.

It would not have escaped Thomas Paine's notice that the oaths contained much regarding allegiance to the House of Hanover and to King George III in particular. The test oath denied the Catholic faith. The oath of abjuration in exhausting detail reified the Hanoverian Court. This oath demanded loyalty to a European royal dynasty, one over the other, which would play out sharply in Paine's later writings, notably *Common Sense*, where Paine ridiculed the idea of monarchy.

Thus began Paine's journey in the Excise Service. The experience could not have been more in contrast to the oaths. Chalmers recorded Paine's first post:

> '*he was soon sent as a supernumerary to gage the brewers of Grantham; and in* **August 1764, he was employed to watch the smugglers of Alford.** *Whether, while he thus walked at Grantham, or rode as an exciseman at Alford, his practises had been misrepresented by malice, or his dishonesty had been detected by watchfulness, tradition has not told us: but it is certain, that he was dismissed from his office, in August, 1765.*'[10]

Chalmers' claim that Paine was taken on as a Supernumerary is confirmed by the actual minute book entry.

Minute Book 1 December 1762

> '*Thomas Middleton, Officer of Holbeach Outride, Grantham Collection, being dead, as by Mr. Thwaites Collector, his letter of 28th.ult. Ordered that the Supernumerary or proper Officer supply the vacancy and that* **Thomas Pain be Supernumerary** *on Mr. Frankland's motion.*'[11]

Before a successful petitioner could become a fully-fledged Officer of Excise he spent time as a Supernumerary on half pay. This could be considered a probationary period where, as described below, the most senior officer in the district could make an assessment of ability.

---

[9] Charles Leadbetter, *The Royal Gauger; Or, Gauging Made Perfectly Easy, as it is Actually Practised by the Officers of His Majesty's Revenue of Excise. In Two Parts*. (London, 1750), p. 214.

[10] Francis Oldys [George Chalmers], *The Life of Thomas Pain; The Author of Rights of Man with a Defence of His Writings* (3rd Edition, London, 1791), p. 19.

[11] The National Archives at Kew (TNA): Public Record Office (PRO), Central Administrative Records of the Board of Excise to 1909, *Excise Board and Secretariat: Minute Books*, CUST47/238, p. 47.

A supernumerary as defined by Leadbetter:

> '*The Supernumerary is a commissioned officer, who attends on the Collector, carries the Portmantua from Place to Place during the Round; receives Half-pay; and when a vacancy happens he goes into business: As soon as that happens the Collector acquaints the Board, and they immediately order him another Supernumerary, who receives his Commission when he comes to the Collector.*'[12]

According to Chalmers, Paine was sent to Grantham in August 1764. There is no actual minute book entry to show when Paine was promoted to Officer status. The minute book entry showing Paine as a Supernumerary was made on 1 December 1762. It must be assumed that Paine spent a long time with the Collector, some 18 months, before he was promoted. Paine was only a fully-fledged Officer of Excise for one year before the minute book showed him as being ordered to be discharged.

Paine's Discharge from the service: Minute Book 27 August 1765:

> '*Thomas Pain, Officer of Alford Outride, Grantham Collection, having on July the 11th stamped his whole Ride as appears by the specimens not being signed in any part thereof though the proper entry was shown in the Journal and the victuallers stocks drawn down in his books as if the same had been surveyed by him that day; as by William Swallow Supervisor's letter of the 3rd instant and the collectors report thereon, also by the said Pain's own confession by letter of the 13th instant;* **ORDERED that he be discharged,** *that Robert Peat dropped malt assistant in Lynn Collection succeed him or &c.*'[13]

Hindmarch was critically suspicious of this last entry.[14] He pointed out that for such a serious offence the entry was very brief. Normally for an offence of this magnitude the details were tediously described. Paine's letter of confession does not survive; it was not transcribed into the minute book and there is no record of it having been forwarded to the board. It could merely have been described by Collector Birdsworth in a covering report.

It could be that Chalmers kept the letter after finding it. Chalmers was indefatigable in his researches; painstaking and accurate in his preparation, he

---

[12] Charles Leadbetter, *The Royal Gauger; Or, Gauging Made Perfectly Easy, as it is Actually Practised by the Officers of His Majesty's Revenue of Excise. In Two Parts.* (London, 1750), p. 220.

[13] TNA: PRO, CUST 47/251, p. 98.

[14] George Hindmarch, 'Thomas Paine: The First Excise Period' (two versions, unpublished, East Sussex Records Offices, The Keep, ACC 10140/2).

went directly to the source for his information.[15] Whilst we can be thankful to him for his assiduous research, Chalmers was noted for having a serious flaw. Public officers took a casual attitude towards state papers, often taking them home and not returning them.[16] There is evidence that Chalmers was guilty of this, since state documents often appear in his papers. This may explain some of the missing letters and Excise records relating to Thomas Paine, to which Chalmers would have been given full access. His comment that *'his practises had been misrepresented by malice'* is a rare acknowledgement that Paine may have been unfairly treated; as this statement does not fit with the generally damning tenor of the biography, there must have been proof.

More recently, Hindmarch forensically proved that Paine had indeed been subject to a false allegation; the evidence that he produced from the Excise minute books would stand up in a court of law today. William Swallow was Paine's supervisor whilst he was an Out Rider at Alford. William Birdsworth was the Collector at Grantham. Both were guilty of unfairly prosecuting the junior officer of the offence in the first instance. The corruption that Hind-march described in his article, *The First Excise Period*,[17] was endemic throughout the Excise Service. Hindmarch covered all these factors in this article; the long-standing corruption was deeply ingrained in the service. Some of the practise was of individual laziness and greed, as in Swallow's case. He was demoted less than seven weeks after Paine's dismissal. The very long entry in the minute book showed the detail normally used when disciplinary action was taken, that the offences Swallow committed were made over a long period of time, and that Paine's orderly books were improperly amended by Swallow.[18] Birdsworth in the first instance, using the convention at the time, colluded with Swallow in felling the junior officer, in part to hide his mismanagement of Swallow.

The full minute entry is transcribed below to show the length and detail in comparison with Paine's short minute of discharge:

> *'William Swallow, Supervisor of Horncastle District, Grantham Collection, having in Alford Outride Officer's 5th and 6th Rounds Book December 17 8 p.m. shown a guile of strong wort but omitted to signify whether any small wort was made, or not till after the columns were dashed off, when he wrote "no small wort" above the dotted lines although there was then small wort doponding and by the same book it ap-*

---

[15] G. A. Cockcroft, *The Public Life of George Chalmers* (New York, 1939), p. 39.

[16] G. A. Cockcroft, *The Public Life of George Chalmers* (New York, 1939), p. 39.

[17] George Hindmarch, 'Thomas Paine: The First Excise Period' (two versions, unpublished, East Sussex Records Offices, The Keep, ACC 10140/2).

[18] TNA: PRO, CUST 47/252, pp. 48-49.

pears to be accounted for by the Officer on his line of survey on January 4th when he showed No. 4 content 23 gallons, full of small in stock and brought it forward in charge, and the said Swallow having in order to cover his neglect wrote of the Officer's said survey, as if wrote by the officer, "No 4 brought on with Certificate and therefore charged" as appears by comparing the handwriting; having on July 22nd accounted for surveying the said Officer's whole short Ride consisting of one victualler, two coffee dealers, and one beer dealer, by check, when he had the Officer's books in his pocket which method of surveying was not only irregular but thereby he had an opportunity of making his surveys agree with the Officer's books before he entered them in his check; and by **Mr. Birdsworth Collector, who was ordered to inquire into the truth of these complaints,** *having reported that the victualler on page 51 says that he did brew some beer on December 17th and turned part thereof into No. 4, and that the said* **Swallow acknowledged that he had the Officer's books in his pocket while he surveyed part of the said Ride and Check; Ordered that he be reduced to be Officer of Hertford 2nd. division, Hertford Collection,** *that William Newton be Supervisor Horncastle District.'[19]*

As Paine was the only riding officer there at that time, it must have Paine's book that Swallow altered. The cited offence happened well before Paine was discharged, meaning that Swallow was committing serious offences for a long time, whilst Paine was in post. This would have been noticed by Paine and the Office Keeper, Solomon Hansord. Someone complained directly to the Commissioners of Excise after Paine's discharge. Hindmarch suggested that Hansord would have known enough to be able to report Swallow's wrongdoing. It was common practice for the Excise Service to keep their office at a local inn. The inn used in Alford was called The Windmill. Hansord was The Windmill's landlord and part-time Office Keeper for the Excise. He had held this post for five years and would have known intimately the comings and goings of the one officer at Alford, Thomas Paine, and the local Supervisor, Swallow. Hansord would have held the key to the Excise strongbox, from which Swallow would have taken Paine's books. Paine lodged at The Windmill, and would have known Hansord well. Thus, Paine would have known Swallow was using and altering his ride books. After a complaint was made by Hansord directly to the Commissioners at the Excise Head Office in Broad Street, London, Birdsworth had to deal with the problem.

Hindmarch described the tightly bound protocol of deference and procedure in the hierarchy of the Excise Service. There were conventions allowing a reasonably swift restoration to service if not too much fuss was made about being discharged, even if it was unfair. In any case, it was impossible for a junior officer to make a complaint about a Supervisor. Birdsworth was a novice Col-

---

[19] TNA: PRO, CUST 47/252, p. 46.

lector, whereas Swallow was practised at bending the rules. Edicts from the Commissioners were made to address the malpractice of superiors using subordinate officers to undertake their own duties.

Hindmarch, by inspecting minute entries and general letters to and from the head office, developed an understanding of the difficulties that am Out Ride Officer faced in the day-to-day execution of his duty. The offence of stamping was that of recording in the Out Ride Officer's own book that a visit to and inspection of a premises had been made when in fact no visit had been made. There were many reasons that the site record belonging to the premises owner might not have been signed. Sometimes the business owner was too busy serving customers, a common situation at brewing ale houses. The business owner might not have been on the premises, and the books might have been kept in the owner's private rooms, which the Out Ride Officer had no legal right to enter. For the offence that Paine was accused of, that of stamping his ride, it was finally recognised by the Commissioners that there were too many reasons that the officer might not have been able to sign a trader, brewer, or distiller's books to match his own records on the day the visit was made.

The struggle to eliminate Ride stamping was finally dispensed with by a **general letter on 23 July 1768**:

> 'The Commissioners upon reconsidering the Nature and Effects of the Instructions contained in the following Clause of General Letter of 27th of February last, viz.
>
> "That they compare the Specimens with the Books in the next Round after the Books are closed and report such other Irregularities and Omissions as they find therein on a spare Leaf at the End of their respective Diaries for that Round"
>
> Order you to cancel the same in every General Letter Book in your Collection into which it hath been copied, It being no longer required that the same be observed.'[20]

Hindmarch concluded that the Board of Commissioners came to realise that unsigned specimens were being exploited unfairly by Supervisors when reporting on Officers.

The difficulties that the Excise Service faced in the 18c were myriad. It is obvious that discipline was required, but at the same time there was not an endless supply of candidates capable of the extremely difficult job of being an Officer of Excise. The corruptions were legend and born of many factors. Most

---

[20] George Hindmarch, 'Thomas Paine: The First Excise Period' (two versions, unpublished, East Sussex Records Offices, The Keep, ACC 10140/2), p. 26.

of the Commissioners were place-men, not professional administrators. Whilst the organisation was the most advanced of its kind in the world, these were early days in terms of a nationwide administration. An example of how common it was to be discharged can be found in the Gauging handbook, the Excise Service's bible of sorts. The author of the 500-page tome was himself discharged:

> '*The true Reason and Grounds of* **my Discharge** *was this. Upon Sunday the 9th of August,* **Thomas Brooks, Officer at Henley- Arden, came to me at Alchurch very drunk; he said that he and I must change Divisions,** *but brought me no note either from the Collector or Supervisor: For these Reasons I told him our Sitting was next Tuesday, and the I should have Orders from them, if it was so. He stayed and dined with me, and* **went home far from being sober; and told his Supervisor, Mr Anthony Gelder, that I refused to remove; which was actually false.** *Since the* **undeserved Treatment** *I have met with, may possibly be of Service to others, I could not think it proper to make it public.*
>
> *In witness to the Truth hereof, I have hereunto put Hand this 24th Day of June 1738.*

Charles Leadbetter'[21]

Along with all the detailed instructions about being an Officer of Excise at every level is the account of his own unfair discharge. Charles Leadbetter was addressing the Officers of Excise directly in this account: it was not for the public. Throughout the minute books there are many accounts of officers being discharged and restored to service, or demoted and later promoted again. It was a fluid situation reflecting both the limited pool of talent and the need for high standards of competency and moral judgement. The tensions that were built into the system from top to bottom – a rigid class system, the primacy of patronage over ability and, as we will find out later, low pay – constantly caused problems. In addition to these internal difficulties, an Out Ride Officer's life was further removed from ease by his environment. Not allowed to practise in their own area, they were removed from their own county, thus losing any family support. The days were long and arduous, and they were often not made welcome by the traders they visited. Smuggling was a real and present daily danger, as many Officers worked in remote areas. Alford was one such place in the Grantham Collection; in 1775 the Collector at Grantham reported to the board that:

---

[21] Charles Leadbetter, *The Royal Gauger; Or, Gauging Made Perfectly Easy, as it is Actually Practised by the Officers of His Majesty's Revenue of Excise. In Two Parts.* (London, 1750), p. 220.

'.....*many of the traders in all the Districts of the said Collection lie very remote from the residences of the Supervisors, that the roads in many places are deep and frequently rendered impassable by being covered with water.....'[22]*

Paine's letter appealing for restoration to the Excise Service:

The text of a letter to the board written on 3 July 1766 by Paine has survived, published by Richard Carlile in 1917, in which Paine appealed for restoration to the service.

> **'London July 3rd 1766**
> *Honourable Sirs,*
>
> *In Humble obedience to your honors' letter of discharge bearing date August 29 1765. I delivered up my commission and since then have given you no trouble. I confess the justice of your honors' displeasure and humbly beg to add my thanks for the candour and lenity with which at that unfortunate time indulged me. And though the nature of the report and my own confession cut off all expectations of enjoying your honors' favor then, yet I humbly hope has not finally excluded me therefrom, upon which hope I humbly presume to entreat your honors to restore me.* **The time I enjoyed my former commission was short and unfortunate- an officer for only a single year. No complaint of the least dishonesty or intemperance ever appeared against me;** *and if I am so happy as to succeed in this my humble petition, I will endeavour that my future conduct shall as much engage your honors' approbation as my former has merited your displeasure.*
>
> **I am, your honors' most dutiful humble servant, Thomas Paine.'**[23]

Hindmarch noted that Paine's claim **'No complaint of the least dishonesty or intemperance ever appeared against me'** was the only part of that appeal that showed Paine's character. Restoration was swift, for the rest of the letter was written in the kind of language that would gain him readmission. The next day's **minute book entry, 4 July 1766:**

> '*Thomas Paine, late officer of Alford Outride Grantham Collection having petitioned to Board praying to be restored, begging Pardon for the*

---

[22] TNA: PRO, CUST 47/299, p. 112.

[23] George Hindmarch, 'Paine at the Crossroads, 1763-1768', *Journal of Radical History*, vol. 9, no. 4 (published posthumously, 2009), p. 4. Moncure Daniel Conway, *The Life of Thomas Paine*, vol. 1 (London, 1909), p. 17.

Offence for which he was Discharged and promising diligence in future;
Ordered that he be restored on a proper vacancy.'[24]

In perhaps a different hand, undated, in reduced script with no punctuation an added note to the above minute entry:

'*he has had notice.*'

The address at the top of Paine's letter of appeal was simply 'London.' Hindmarch suggested that he wrote it from within the Excise Office in Broad Street and that the letter was written after an enquiry was made by Paine directly to Mr. Earle, the official in charge of those matters. Earle would have known the details of Paine's previous unfair dismissal, and guided him in the language that he should use to the Commissioners. The language that was used in Paine's application for restoration was carefully worded to show deference and subservience: appropriate language for a structured, class-defined organisation. The speedy restoration, made the next day, indicates that the appeal was immediately dealt with.

On Friday 15 of May 1767 Paine was '**restored on a proper vacancy**':

> '*George Chappell Officer of Grampound Dvn. Cornwall Collection, having been ill ever since the 25th of February last & unlikely to do business again, as by John Hewett Supervisor's Letter of the 10th inst. ORDERED that he relinquish & have leave to qualify for the Charity; and that Thomas Pain who was discharged & is restored succeed him.*'[25]

On Saturday the 30th of May 1767 Paine '**prayed leave to wait another vacancy**':

> '*Thomas Pain, restored, who by minute of the 15th inst. was appointed officer of Grampound Dvn. Cornwall Collection* **having prayed leave to wait another Vacancy**; *ORDERED that William Barnes, who was discharged & is restored, be officer of Grampound Dvn. in his stead.*'
> '*see Pain's letter of the 26th inst.*'[26]

Paine's letter of the 26th has not been found to date, nor do we have exact knowledge of how Paine spent the time between his restoration on 3 of July 1766 until the offer the vacancy at Grampound on 15 July 1767. Very little detail is known about Paine's movement and occupation during his two inter-

---

24 TNA: PRO, CUST 47/255, p. 87.

25 TNA: PRO, CUST 47/258, p. 106.

26 TNA: PRO, CUST 47/259, p. 10.

im periods from Excise duty. Chalmers recorded that Paine taught for Mr. Noble, who *'kept the great Academy in Lemon Street'*,[27] after his restoration until Christmas 1766 and then for Mr. Gardnor at a reputable school at Kensington for the first three months of 1767. Chalmers also stated that Paine *'preached in Moorfields and in various populous places in England'* but there is no other evidence of Paine preaching at this time.[28]

The next entry regarding Paine's progress in the Excise, the minute book entry on 18 February 1768:

> *'.....that Dan Jones Officer of Wells Out Ride Taunton Collection succeed him at his own request;* & **that Tho. Paine, who was discharged & is restored succeed Jones.'**[29]

Paine, due to changing circumstances, never took up his post at Wells, as indicated in the minute book entry on 29 February 1768:

> *'Notwithstanding the minute of the 18th inst. whereby Daniel Jones Officer of Wells Out Ride Collection was appointed Officer of Abergavenny 1 Out Ride Wales East Collection; it is now ORDERED that he continue Officer of Wells Out Ride till another Vacancy, that Richard Dalton Officer of Lewes 4 Out Ride Sussex Collection be Officer of Abergavenny 1 Out Rode at his own request;* & **that Thomas Paine, who by the Minute was appointed Officer of Wells Out Ride be Officer of Lewes 4 Out Ride.'**[30]

Thomas Paine soon arrived in Lewes, where he was to spend the next six years. Paine fully engaged with this unusual county town, where he debated, married, went into business, and, most importantly for this story, wrote *'The Case of the Officers of Excise.'*

One more entry appeared for Thomas Paine in the minute book right at the end of his time in Lewes, a sad entry that he probably never saw. This will be shown in the conclusion to highlight the complications that this radical thinker must have endured due to his efforts to help his king and country.

---

[27] Francis Oldys [George Chalmers], *The Life of Thomas Pain; The Author of Rights of Man with a Defence of His Writings* (3rd Edition, London, 1791), p. 20.

[28] Francis Oldys [George Chalmers], *The Life of Thomas Pain; The Author of Rights of Man with a Defence of His Writings* (3rd Edition, London, 1791), p. 21.

[29] TNA: PRO, CUST 47/262, p. 8.

[30] TNA: PRO, CUST 47/262, p. 24.

CHAPTER 5

Corruption in the Excise Service reached a breaking point

The fact that Paine prayed leave to wait for another vacancy rather than take up his post in Grampound in the Cornwall Collection might mean one of two things. It could be that he was considering another course of occupation. Or it could be that notice had come to him of just how corrupt the Excise Service in Grampound was at that time. An extraordinary minute book entry was read out to all the Commissioners on **Tuesday 12 July 1768** regarding the Cornwall Collection. The litany of offences occupied 20 pages of the minute book detailing just about every offence that could be made. The extremely long catalogue of serious misdemeanours had been going on for a long time, well before Paine was ordered to be an officer in Grampound Division, Cornwall Collection. The long entry starts on page 90 with:

> *'Giles Moore, supervisor of Bodmyn District Cornwall Collection, having on the 6th of may not sent up the first, second, third and 4th Round books to the office, tho the first of these books should have been sent at the end of the third round, viz in December last....having not changed the letters of the Hide Stamps in many of the divisions so frequently as he ought have done.......having surveyed but little by check.....**having not made a Total in his Diary book of the miles and traders surveyed each day....'** ORDERED be reduced from Supervisor to Officer Stourbridge 8th Division in Wolverhampton Collection.'*[31]

The list of at least twenty offences that Moore committed went on over three pages. The next in line for discipline:

> *'John Hewitt Supervisor of Truro District Cornwall Collection, having not completed the schemes of Traders Entries in check...having kept no account of the Fairs in the District....having not been attentive in gauging....in Truro Dvn 1st 2nd & 3rd Out Ride Redruth Division and 2nd Out Ride, Tregony Division and 1st Out Ride and Grampound Division*

---

[31] TNA: PRO, CUST 47/263, pp. 91, 93.

*Instances of neglect in Gauging...having not once surveyed by Check 159 victuallers in Tregony Division, 14 in in Truro Out Ride....***having one of his officers say to his knowledge never having changed the letters in his Hide Stamp since he has been in the Division which is thirteen years ....Ordered that he be Discharged.'**[32]

Hewitt had committed more offences over a longer period of time and in the very division that Paine was destined for in Grampound, hence the discharge. Next to be reprimanded was:

*'John Dewick Supervisor of Launceston District Cornwall Collection, having the scheme of Traders Entries in Check incorrect....having surveyed by Check in Camelford Division only Thrice, in Launceston Division twice, in Millbrook Division once....having not furnished his officers with the latest Malt Act.....having suffered the officer Launceston Division to stock by sound a cask of Rum containing above One Hundred Gallons, which in that smuggling Country gives an opening for fraud.....having permitted some of his officers to sell condemned spirits by contract with Traders and other persons...***Ordered that the said Dewick be reduced to Officer of Lewes 1st Division Sussex Collection.'**[33]

These entries are much truncated due to the number of offences and their technical nature. That each entry went over many pages is a distinctive feature of the corrupt Supervisors, Officers, and Examiners in Cornwall. Note that the numerous charges made against Hewitt and Dewick (and Shute, below) only resulted in demotion. This is in contrast to the one charge made against Paine in Alford causing his discharge. Dewick was sent to Lewes, where Paine was already in post. The next Supervisor in Cornwall to be excoriated over a three-page diatribe of serious offences:

*'Henry Shute Supervisor of Helston District Cornwall Collection having several times taken Common Brewers Drink into the stocks of brewing victuallers from another without certificates, whereby his Officers have been misguided, & done the same.....having not sworn a chandler in St Ives Out Ride to any of his entries from the 21st February to the 21st of November....having not furnished the Officer of Marketjow Division with brandy instructions.....Entries copied from the Officers which are so erroneous that they cannot be depended upon in Check Surveying......having suffered his officers to sell Condemned Spirits by private contract with their Traders and other persons in their divisions instead of selling them by auction in a public sale....***having neglected to Report the sev-**

---

[32] TNA: PRO, CUST 47/263, pp. 94-98.

[33] TNA: PRO, CUST 47/263, pp. 98, 100.

eral faults found upon his Officers.....ORDERED be Reduced to be Officer of Cambridge 4th Division Cambridge Collection.'[34]

Over four pages of the minute book, starting with page 104, the top man, the Collector for Cornwall, was brought to justice:

> **'Mr Richard Baker Collector of Cornwall Collection** *having suffered the Supervisors of Truro & Bodmin Districts to be very negligent.......the check of Truro District to be very imperfect.....having not shown several of his supervisors and officers the particulars of the charges of condemned seizures.....having suffered several of his officers both in Out Ride and Town Walks to bring to the sitting the Duty for the Bulk of the Traders under their Survey, whereby they have had considerable sums of money in their hands, notwithstanding the Boards repeated Orders to the contrary......***and having the whole business of his supervisors throughout his Collection to be performed in a careless inattentive manner insomuch that one of them is Discharged and the other three Reduced: ORDERED that Richard Baker be Discharged.'**[35]

It would be too tedious to transcribe all twenty pages of minute book entries describing the complete collapse of the Cornwall Collection. The above excerpts alone show how deep the corruption was in the entire county of Cornwall at every level of the Excise Service. That the Excise Commissioners could lose control over such a very long time in a such large collection was very serious indeed. That the Collector and one Supervisor were discharged and three Supervisors were reduced must have sent tremors right through the service. Just about every rule was broken in Cornwall. The transgressions were wholesale, and the 20 pages of detailed reasons for discipline must have required people on the ground to report on every aspect. This means that many Officers or Office Keepers must have been encouraged to report on their superiors, as may have happened in Alford in Swallow's case, in which Paine was unfairly discharged. Paine may have been encouraged to report on Swallow. There must have been a real concern at Board level; for the Commissioners, being read out these twenty pages detailing the disastrous behaviour in Cornwall energised a desire in them to somehow solve the problem of corruption.

---

[34] TNA: PRO, CUST 47/263, pp. 100, 103.

[35] TNA: PRO, CUST 47/263, pp. 104, 107.

CHAPTER 6

The national campaign

It is a real journey of discovery to go through the Treasury Boxes at the National Archives at Kew. The material in these boxes, kept under the general classification of T1, is arranged by date, but is not classified. When a box is called up from the deep of the archive, one does not know what is inside. This can be as frustrating as it is exciting; many boxes often have to be trawled through before one can find the object of desire, if it exists at all. During this search to find documents relevant to *The Case of the Officers of Excise*, earlier petitions came to light which appealed for higher pay for Excise Officers.

The Case of the Officers of Excise will be discussed later, but to date, although *The Case* has been known about for a long time now, the petition with signatures from 3,000 Excise Officers that was supposedly attached was considered missing. It was considered that Paine wrote the first and only appeal for better pay and conditions. The discovery of earlier petitions has now changed that view. The signatures attached to the earlier petitions are almost definitely some of the signatures that Paine referred to later.

It can be seen from the Cornwall Collection that the myriad problems emanating from corruption had completely come to light. Previously, if an officer were to report corruption, even by an anonymous source, is was the lowest officer in service that would be discharged. An earlier example was shown with Swallow and Birdsworth's treatment of Paine. In this case, it was Paine who lost his job first. Not the Supervisor who, in Swallow's case, was certainly involved in illegal practice. Paine had to go, but evidence came out later that caused Swallow also to lose his position.

In Cornwall, however, it was the Supervisors and the Collector who were either demoted or discharged. In a twenty-page minute entry, these higher-ranking officers were summarily dealt with in one sitting in London. There must have been a concentrated effort to collect the evidence that was cited in this minute entry in order to prove that the Supervisors and the Collector were complicit in the corruption. The ordinary Excise Officers escaped censure, although they must have been the ones who reported the detailed transgressions, implying that they might have been involved; no other people would have known the details of the regulations, and corrupt traders would hardly have spoiled attractive arrangements.

There was an exquisite tension at play. The craft of gauging was a rare skill, a competency that was not available to everyone. An innate ability for numeracy followed by rigorous application was required to reach qualification. Only a small percentage of the population of England could actually do this job. It had to be the Commissioners of Excise who directed the operation to root out the corruption. No one else was separated from the corruption in the same way. There were nine Commissioners who were paid a salary of £1000 per annum each. This was compared to 3,175 Country and London Officers who each received an annual pay, after reductions, of £46. The petitions specifically cited the gross salary of £50, thus excluding every other rank above (253 Country Supervisors earned £90 and 53 Country Collectors £120 per annum) and below (52 Supernumeraries earned £25 per annum).[36] Therefore, it was the front-line officers who laboured under almost impossible conditions, as the wording in the petitions laid out. It was a mathematical problem. The revenue was compromised by corruption. To root corruption out required careful consideration. The Commissioners knew that mass discharge of corrupt officers would collapse the entire service; there was simply not enough talent readily available to replace them.

The root of the problem was the very low pay that caused the corruption in the first place. A strategy in Cornwall was put into play in order to expose the corruption: punish those who should know better and were being paid more, the Supervisors and Collectors, and at the same time make a concerted and reasoned appeal for higher pay to the Treasury, the only group who could grant this. It must have taken a long time to collect the evidence to root out the corruption in Cornwall Collection. A system of reporting must have been put into place that protected the informants, the Division and Out Ride Officers.

George Lewis Scott was now the senior board member, having been appointed in 1758.[37] Graham Smith, the librarian and archivist of HM Customs and Excise, noted that it was not until the mid-1700's that able administrators served as Commissioners of Excise, and that George Lewis Scott, who was a distinguished mathematician, brought new ideas to the board.[38] Scott was singled out by Smith as being the exception to the rule. Most previous appointees were granted their positions based on privilege rather than merit; unless they

---

[36] TNA: PRO, CUST 48/12. List of the several officers Established officers in the Revenue of Excise under Our Management distinguishing their respective Salaries and appointments: pp. 120-125 in the Entry books of Correspondence with the Treasury.

[37] W. A. Speck, *A Political Biography of Thomas Paine* (London, 2013).

[38] Graham Smith, *Something to Declare: 1000 years of Customs and Excise* (London, 1980).

behaved badly, they held the appointment for life. It appears that the anti-corruption campaign was at the heart of Scott's new thinking.

The Missing Signatures

Finding these two documents in the Treasury Boxes revealed, for the first time, the missing signatures. In a later letter to Oliver Goldsmith, Paine claimed a signed petition accompanied *The Case of The Officers of Excise:*

> 'A Petition for this purpose has been circulated thro' every part of the Kingdom, and signed by all the officers therein.'

To date, none of these signatures had come to light, so they were considered missing.

The two documents together represent five collections. Wales was divided into four collections, East, West, North, and South, plus Hereford. Finding these documents provided not only some of the missing signatures but also showed the deep procedure and logic of the campaign. The petition documents are both on one large sheet, and the text is copied out in a fair hand with the bottom half lined and divided to place the signatures of the Officers of Excise. They are all Out Ride or Division Officers. There are 79 signatures on the earlier petition. The petition is written out at the head of the document, which was presumably then taken round so that each officer could read and then sign the document. The officers signed in one column and wrote their division or out ride in the column adjacent to it.

The title face of the first document from Wales read:

'Officers of the Revenues of Excise in ~~Scotland~~ Wales Memorial for additional Pay

Received 17th January 1769.'[39]

The mistake in the title of the first petition is an indication of central control. Scotland would not have been written in error if the document emanated from Wales. This mistake strongly suggests that there were several of these templates. Additionally, the wording in the petition is generic, with no particular region mentioned.

The petition from the Excise Officers of Wales on 17 January 1769:

---

[39] TNA: PRO, T1 470/283-284.

'To The Right Honourable The Lords Commissioners of the Treasury

The humble Petition of the Officers of his Majesties Revenues of Excise, Malt, and other Duties under the management of the Commissioners of Excise

Most humbly sheweth

That the high price of provisions has at last reduced your Petitioners to the necessity of laying their Case before your Lordships, not doubting but when your Lordships shall be made acquainted with their poor and needy circumstances, you will humanely consider their situation and be pleased to appoint some addition to their present scanty allowance of pay.

Your Petitioners beg leave humbly to set forth to your Lordships that their salary was established at fifty Pounds per annum. That it has continued ever since without the least addition: on the other hand it has been lowered that now the poor Office hath paid the Civil List, the Charity, the Sittings, & other expenses which are unavoidable in the execution of his Office, he hath not more than forty six per annum to provide himself and wife together with a large family, to pay for Horse-keeping, House-rent, firing and other articles which are absolutely necessary for the support of Life.

Your Petitioners have laboured under great Hardships for a long time past without troubling your Lordships, hoping that provisions would soon come cheaper- but in vain – they find poverty daily bearing harder and harder upon them and have great Reason to fear, that (without the merciful interposition of your Lordships) very few of them can be able to weather out these times, for their poverty will deter people of upright and humane principles from assisting them till the necessaries of Life shall be more reasonable, there being so very little likelihood of their having it in their Power ever to make them satisfaction.

They will be under the necessity often of applying to persons who will make an advantage of their circumstances, for none will relieve them, but designing men, who have some Views of Gain thereby. They indeed under the cover of charity may lend an officer some assistance, which the cries of a starving family may urge him (tho' reluctantly) to accept of.

And When he has so done he can no longer do as his Duty requires; for altho' he may see or know of any Practices carried on by such persons detrimental to the Revenue, he dares not complain to his superior thereof, because he very well knows that he holds his office but at the mercy of those men, and must therefore pass it over in silence, or have the dependence of himself and Family at once cut off.

Your Petitioners therefore most humbly implore your Lordships to take into consideration the premises, and to grant such Relief therein as to your Lordships shall seem Meet and your Petitioners as in Duty shall ever pray.'[40]

It would have taken a national strategy to circulate a single document, signed by every Officer throughout Wales and beyond, wherein one of the main points was critical of the Supervisors who would have been charged with that circulation. The petitions would have had to be presented to officers at sitting days in the various towns on the day when Supervisors would have been present. It is unthinkable that this was done in secret. It would have been unworkable for any other mechanism other than that of an instruction from the Commissioners to the Collector and then to the Supervisors to get the petition round these vast areas and get them signed. It could be that due to the severity of the corruption, and the impending disciplinary action, the Collector and the Supervisors had warning not to impede this process. It might be a mistake to think that it was pure admonishment from above, though. It was more likely a collaborative effort. The collection of a signature and, as Paine stated, three shillings for the cost of printing the final version of *The Case* from every officer in England would have been very difficult without cooperation at all levels. Supervisors and Collectors promoted from the Officer ranks would have suffered privation themselves, and perhaps had learnt the art of corruption through necessity.

Excise revenue was under severe threat from one factor: low pay to the majority of officers. Inflation had forced officers to ask for more pay, which had been fixed at £50 for a long time. The salary had also been further diminished, due to deductions for charity and administration, to £46. This amount was too small to support a large family and to subsist horse keeping, house rent, fires in winter and food.

The next petition from the rest of the officers of Wales had written on the front of the petition: **'Wales and Hereford'** on **30 June 1769.**

The message contained in this petition varied in detail but not in essence from the earlier one. It was not as well-couched, but the points made were

---

[40] TNA: PRO, T1 470/283-284.

exactly the same as before. Above the list of signatories can be seen written in bold and large **'Hereford Collection,'** which has been very heavily scored out, but some of the signatures are from Hereford, which must be in that collection. There are 179 signatures on this sheet, which is laid out the same way as the January petition. The names and the out rides and divisions are not the same as those from the January submission. The dates on the documents are the dates that they were received into the Treasury department. The documents were folded in such a way to form their own envelope, with the facing page showing the title of what was within.

On the second petition, to the side and bottom of the signatures is written, *'June the 30th 1769 finished,'*[41] showing that all officers had signed. Both petitions had treasury notes on the back of them acknowledging receipt and that they were from the *'English Excise.'*

Both appeals were sent directly to the Lords of the Treasury. Accompanying the second petition from Wales was an unsigned and undated letter. The letter made it clear that the Commissioners of Excise had no power to grant the appeal for higher pay. The Treasury was above the Commissioners of Excise in ranking, and importantly made the decision whether to grant funds that were made by any petition. The language used in the discrete petitions made at the top of every list of signatories varied slightly but were the same in intent. Although it was acknowledged that the officers were under the management of the Commissioners of Excise, the submissions went straight to the Lords. There might have been a good reason to leave the Commissioners of Excise out in the first instance. Perhaps it was a device for the Commissioners of Excise to raise awareness without implicating themselves in the process.

There is further evidence for a hands-off approach by the Commissioners in an appeal from the Excise Officers in Scotland, again directly to the Lords of the Treasury in London. There was a separate board of Excise Commissioners in Scotland but the Lords of the Treasury held the purse strings for the whole of the United Kingdom.[42] This petition, signed at the bottom by 29 signatories, concentrated on the fact that the Scottish Excise Officers were paid less than their English counterparts, and was accompanied by a very detailed table of expenses. The note at the bottom of the list of expenses made the point about corruption in a different way:

> *'By the above calculations it will be obvious that Scotch Excise Officers live at present in a very scanty and mean way, as they are obliged to retrench about a fourth part of every article.*

---

[41] TNA: PRO, T1 470/283-284.

[42] Graham Smith, *Something to Declare: 1000 years of Customs and Excise* (London, 1980), p. 34.

The officers in the same revenue in England and Ireland have much better encouragement tho' it is well known that all the necessities of life are now as dear on Scotland as in most parts of the former, and much higher in the latter.

Whether it be for the INTEREST of the REVENUE that those who serve in it be allowed what will maintain a tolerable decency to screen them from the insult, and put them above the VULGAR, and to attend to the diligent and faithful execution of their office, is most humbly submitted to those in power. *[signed] J Cummins Officer of Excise in Edinburgh Buchanan Officer of Excise in Glasgow for themselves and Brethren.'*[43]

The four main complaints contained in all three petitions were that:

- The pay was too low and had been for a long time in the face of inflation
- The pay had been lowered further through deductions for the Civil List and Charity
- The officers lived in poverty and were therefore subject to corruption from traders
- If they complained to a superior or reported corruption they would lose their jobs

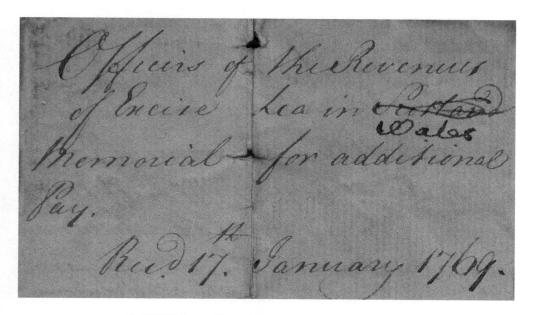

JANUARY 1769 PETITION SHOWING THE ERROR

---

43 TNA: PRO, T1 469/330.

All three petitions were sent directly to the Lords of the Treasury and not to the Commissioners of Excise.

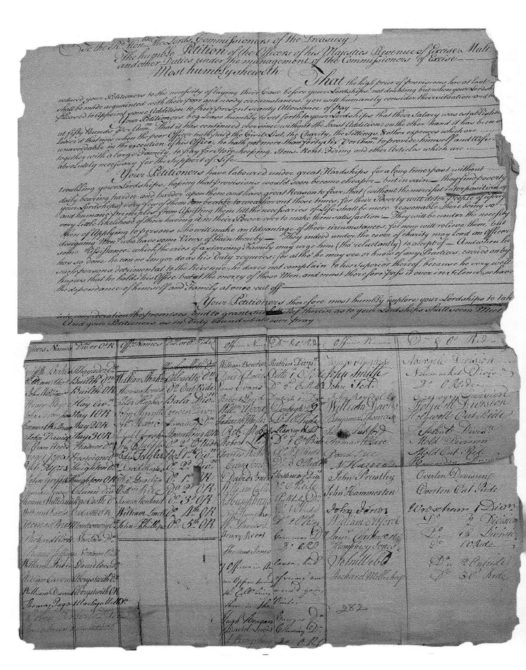

JANUARY 1769 PETITION AND SIGNATURES FROM FOUR COLLECTIONS IN WALES

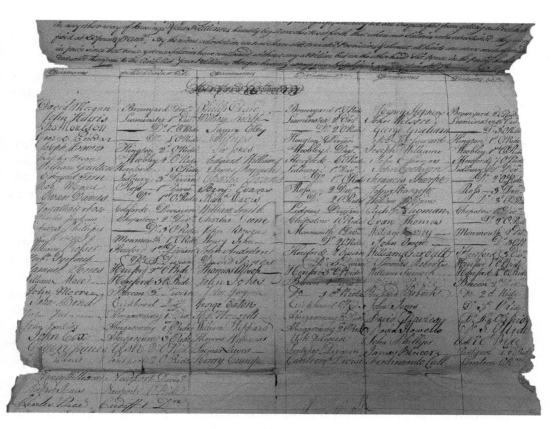

JUNE 1769 PETITION AND SIGNATURES FROM WALES AND HEREFORD

CHAPTER 7

The Case of The Officers of Excise

We now turn to the final part of this national campaign in which Thomas Paine was selected from over 3,000 Officers of Excise to write *The Case*, the full title of which is:

> **'The Case of the Officers of Excise; With Remarks on the Qualifications of Officers and on the Numerous Evils arising to the Revenue. From the Insufficiency of the Present Salary Humbly addressed to the Hon. And Right Hon. the Members of Both Houses of Parliament.'**

The reason why Thomas Paine was selected will probably never be fully known, and will be considered later in the context of moving to Lewes and meeting William Lee, the newspaper owner. There might have been other factors; his earlier visit to the head office of the Excise to apply for restoration could indicate that he was part of an effort to reduce corruption then. As with many facets of history, we are reliant on official records; the quiet, spoken communication is lost for ever. Paine wrote to Oliver Goldsmith after *The Case* was printed. It is possible to interpret this letter in a different way now that signatures in the petitions from Wales have come to light. Before now, it had been taken that Paine was the architect and sole mover of this campaign. Hindmarch had pointed out that this was unlikely. Now that we have considered the problems in Cornwall and the timeline of the action taken by the Commissioners, we can interpret this letter more fully:

Letter from Thomas Paine to Oliver Goldsmith 21 December 1772, written from the Excise Coffee House in Broad Street:

'Honoured Sir

Herewith I present you with a case of the Officers of Excise. A compliment of this kind from an entire stranger may appear somewhat singular; But the following reasons and Informations, will I presume sufficiently apologise.

I act myself in the humble Station of an Officer of Excise tho' somewhat differently circumstanced to what many of them are, and have been the Principal Promoter of a Plan for applying to Parliament this session for an increase of Salary.

A Petition for this purpose has been circulated thro' every part of the Kingdom, and signed by all the officers therein. A subscription of three shillings per Officers is raised, amounting to upwards of five hundred pounds for supporting the expenses. The Excise Officers in all cities and corporate towns have obtained Letters of Recommendation from the Electors to the Members on their behalf, many or most of them have Promised their support. The enclosed Case we have presented to most of the Members and shall to all before the petition appears in the House.

The Memorial before you met with so much approbation while in Manuscript that I was advised to print four thousand copies, Three Thousand copies, Three Thousand of which were subscribed to by the officers in general and the remaining 1000 for presents.

Since delivering them, I have received so many letters of thanks and approbation for the Performance that were I not singularly modest I should insensibly become a little vain.

The literary fame of Dr Goldsmith has induced me to present one to him. Such as it is it is my first and only attempt and even now should not have undertaken it had I not been particularly applied to by some of my superiors in office.

I have a few questions to trouble Dr Goldsmith with and should esteem his company for an hour or two, to partake of a bottle of Wine or anything else, and apologise for this trouble, as a singular favour conferred on

His unknown Humble Servt. and admirer

Thomas Pain

P.S. I shall take the Liberty of waiting on you in a day or two.'[44]

Contrary to many claims over the years, there was never any reply to this letter, nor did they ever meet. During the current research, some time was spent in Oliver Goldsmith's archive in the British Library. This letter is there but there are no other references to Paine. Goldsmith was right in the middle of trying to get *She Stoops to Conquer* on the stage at that time. He died at the age

---

[44] Thomas Paine, 'Letter to Oliver Goldsmith', 21 December 1772, *The Complete Writings of Thomas Paine*, ed. Philip S. Foner, vol. 2 (New York, 1945), p. 1129.

of 46 on 4 April 1774, giving little time for the two men to have met.[45] That Goldsmith had acknowledged gauging as a high art in *The Deserted Village* whilst extolling the village schoolmaster perhaps gave Paine some hope of an audience:

> *'Twas certain he could write, and cypher too;*
> *Lands he could measure, terms and tides presage,*
> *And ev'n the story ran that he could gauge.'*[46]

It is clear that Paine wrote *The Case*, but knowing about the petitions from Wales now makes more sense of his line **'A Petition for this purpose has been circulated thro' every part of the Kingdom, and signed by all the officers therein.'** Whilst Paine claimed authorship of *The Case*, he did not claim to have orchestrated the petition.

The effort that Paine was involved in with his writing of *The Case* had evolved from the earlier presentations of petitions to the Lords. It can now be considered that the strategy of reducing corruption was a developing plan that changed tactic over the years. It can be seen by the distance that just two petitions had to travel geographically that their distribution would have taken a long time. Pain stated that **'A Petition for this purpose has been circulated thro' every part of the Kingdom, and signed by all the officers therein.'** It could not have been just one petition, however. The Wales January 1769 petition had 79 signatures, and the June 1769 had 179 signatures. If we take the larger petition, it is about as big a document as could have been circulated and handled many times in remote places. For 3,000 signatures at a maximum of 179 signatures per document, 17 documents would have had to have been produced centrally and sent all over England. The fact that the first one contained 79 signatures suggests that there were more than 17 produced. It is hard to estimate the time it would take to produce, distribute and deliver these petitions back to London.

The petitions from Wales and Scotland were addressed directly to the Lords of the Treasury. This time the petition was from the committee of eight and was presented to the Commissioners of Excise. This committee was now deputed by the whole body of the Officers of Excise throughout England and Wales. This petition was then forwarded to the Lords of the Treasury by the Excise Commissioners humbly asking them to consider the plea for higher pay. It can be concluded that all petitions were in fact the same petition in essence, as part of the national campaign. The main points covered varied in text but not in meaning. The petitions that headed up the signed documents were hand written and changed slightly in that transcription process but the

---

[45] Gerard A. Lee, 'Oliver Goldsmith', *Dublin Historical Record*, vol. 26, no. 1 (December 1972), p. 17.

[46] Gerard A. Lee, 'Oliver Goldsmith', *Dublin Historical Record*, vol. 26, no. 1 (December 1972), p. 15.

core meaning was the same. Therefore, when Paine claimed that the petition was signed by all the Officers of Excise in England and Wales, this was not a direct reference to the exact petition the committee of eight sent to the Commissioners of Excise but to the petitions, the same in essence, that had been distributed all over the country.

The eight members of the committee were:

Thomas Sykes , officer in the London service, Calicoes Division

William May, officer in the London service, Brandy Distilleries

Henry Holland, an officer in Nottingham

Thomas Gray, officer in the London service, 6th Division Distillery

John Grosse, an officer in Newcastle

Richard Ayling, an officer in the London service, 1st Division Brewery

Thomas Pattinson, an officer in Gravesend and Rochester

Thomas Paine, an officer in the Sussex Collection, Lewes 4th Outride

It would have been an extraordinary feat for anyone not at the centre of operations to assemble seven other Officers of Excise from such a large geographical spread. It was more likely a device constructed to resemble an organisation from below, to disguise the Commissioners' involvement. There is also a strength in numbers, as the committee device diffused responsibility. Paine does not claim that he wrote the petition, although a balance between the petition and *The Case* can be seen. There was no claim of corruption this time; the thrust of the petition was about inflationary forces, expenses and further deductions that had reduced the salary which had been fixed for a long time. No actual figures were stated in this petition. There was an additional complaint in this petition, that as they were removed from their natural friends and families they were deprived of any assistance that might be given from them. This petition claimed to represent all the officers of England and Wales deputed by the committee of eight. There is no mention of mass signatures. This suggests that the signatures of all the nation's officers that Paine mentioned in his letter to Goldsmith were in fact the earlier petitions, some of which we have now seen.

The Case of The Officers of Excise, a pamphlet of 21 pages octavo size, was intended, as Paine stated in his letter to Goldsmith, for all Officers of Excise, members of both Houses of Parliament, and influential people in towns and cities. It is not clear that it was presented for debate or as a supporting

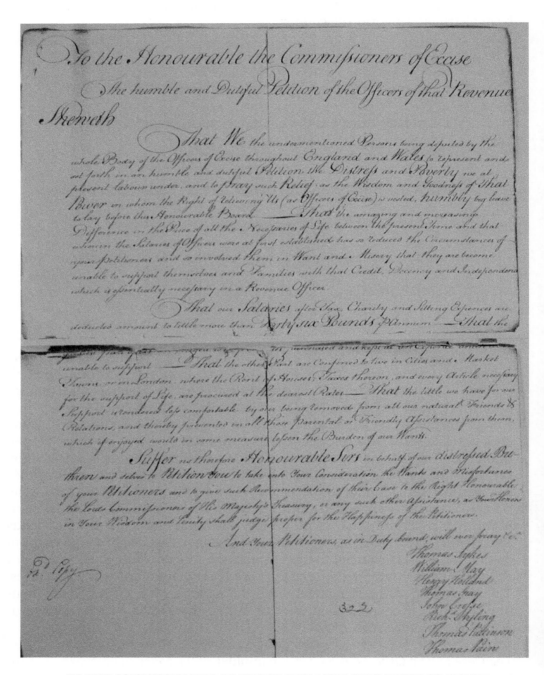

TO THE COMMISSIONERS OF EXCISE FROM THE COMMITTEE OF EIGHT

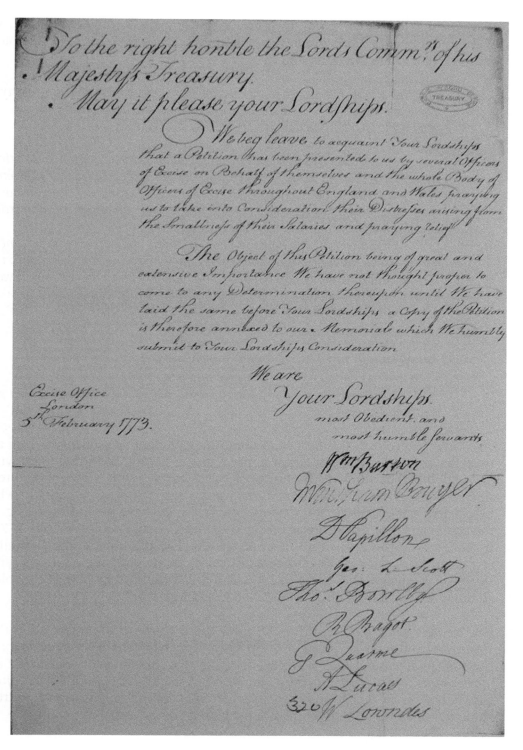

To the right honble the Lords Comm.rs of his Majesty's Treasury.

May it please your Lordships.

We beg leave to acquaint Your Lordships that a Petition has been presented to us by several Officers of Excise on Behalf of themselves and the whole Body of Officers of Excise throughout England and Wales praying us to take into Consideration their Distresses arising from the Smallness of their Salaries and praying relief

The Object of this Petition being of great and extensive Importance We have not thought proper to come to any Determination thereupon until We have laid the same before Your Lordships a Copy of the Petition is therefore annexed to our Memorial which We humbly submit to Your Lordships Consideration

We are
Your Lordships.
most Obedient, and
most humble servants

Excise Office
London
5th February 1773.

TO THE LORDS OF THE TREASURY FROM THE COMMISSIONERS OF
EXCISE

document for the petition. The petition was destined for the Houses of Parliament, but it seems the petition never made it that far. It was sent to the Lords of the Treasury with a covering letter from the Commissioners of Excise on **5 February 1773**, some five weeks after the letter was sent to Goldsmith by Paine. The covering letter:

> '*To the Right Honourable the Lords Commissioners of his Majesty's Treasury*
> *May it please your Lordships*
>
>   *We beg leave to acquaint your Lordships that a Petition has been presented to us by several officers of Excise on behalf of themselves and the whole body of Officers of Excise throughout England and Wales praying us to take into consideration their distresses arising from the smallness of their salaries and praying relief.*
>   *The object of this Petition being of great and extreme importance, we have not thought proper to come to any determination thereupon, till we have laid the same before your Lordships. We have therefore annexed to our Memorial a copy of the Petition which we humbly submit to your Lordships Consideration*
>
>   *We are*
> *Excise Office*   *Your Lordships*
> *5th February 1773*   *most obedient and*
>   *most humble servants*
>   *[s i g n e d   b y   t h e   n i n e   E x c i s e*
> *Commissioners].*'[47]

This time no protocol was spared. A committee of eight was arranged from all over the country. The deputation applied to the Excise Commissioners who forwarded the petition to the Lords of the Treasury with a covering letter. The accompanying pamphlet, *The Case,* was an urgent, deeper account of why higher pay was essential. What happened next must have been devastating to the campaign. The petition was received by the Treasury on 5 February 1773. It was read by the Lords on 9 February 1773. The petitioners, the Commissioners of Excise and all the Officers of Excise, finally had their answer after a five-year campaign: they were to get nothing. Written on the face of the folded document is **'Read Feb. 9. 1773.'** And just below, **'Nil.'**

On the very same day the Prime Minister, Lord North, made a speech in the House of Commons against a petition from captains in the navy '*praying for a reasonable increase of their half pay,*' warning that '*it will open the door for all other claims, which though perhaps not equally founded, are yet not less needful.*' North made it clear that he knew that there was another application from the shipwrights on the way to the House for higher pay:

---

[47] TNA: PRO, T1 501, pp. 322-3.

'And there may be others in the service of government whose wants may be still greater, though their merit may be less, whom pity would wish to relieve in these times of general distress; it is therefore the absolute impossibility of complying with all applications that induces me to oppose the present.'[48]

One of those applications was from the Officers of Excise. North's speech in parliament killed the Excise campaign stone dead. It scuppered the plan to present the petition to government; there is no record of it ever being presented.[49] There is no record of pamphlet, *The Case of The Officers of Excise*, either being officially received or distributed either. Chalmers noted that *'Four Thousand of The Case were printed by Mr William Lee of Lewes, in 1772. But even the copies, which were intended for the members of parliament, not all were distributed.'*[50] The campaign was over.

A world first, the campaign culminating in *The Case* represented a national organisation of workers, their voice articulated in one document. The pamphlet echoed the themes of the petitions from Wales and Scotland. It was initiated from within the government, not from the very top but very close to it.

It came from the administrators who had to deal with everyday corruption, rife through the entire service. There was a carefully thought out assessment of the problem, resulting in action that was calculated to solve it.

Scant attention has been paid to this pamphlet. Chalmers noted that *'On these topics he says all that the ablest writer could have said.'* After some of the usual negative comments he continued, *'his first pamphlet will be considered as his best performance by all those, who regard truth as superior to falsehood, modesty to imprudence, and just complaint to factious innovation.'*[51] Perhaps Chalmers had some sympathy for *The Case;* he was a civil servant himself and had experienced the iniquities of being in service at a lower level, although it is hard to discern if Chalmers just used this as an opportunity to malign Paine's later writing, in particular *The Rights of Man.*[52] J.S. Jordan published a copy of *The*

---

[48] Great Britain Parliament: House of Commons, *The Debates and Proceedings of the British House of Commons, From April 1772 to July 1773* (London, 1774), pp. 196-200.

[49] W. A. Speck, *A Political Biography of Thomas Paine* (London, 2013), p. 22.

[50] Francis Oldys [George Chalmers], *The Life of Thomas Pain; The Author of Rights of Man with a Defence of His Writings* (3rd Edition, London, 1791), p. 29.

[51] Francis Oldys [George Chalmers], *The Life of Thomas Pain; The Author of Rights of Man with a Defence of His Writings* (3rd Edition, London, 1791), pp. 28-29.

[52] G. A. Cockcroft, *The Public Life of George Chalmers* (New York, 1939), p. 129.

Case in 1793 in full with a preface by an unknown author. The preface does not analyse *The Case,* rather using it as an indication of the ability of Thomas Paine to write, and then mentioning much of his later writing. George Hindmarch was the first to attempt to partly analyse *The Case.* All other biographies have tended to gloss over *The Case, perhaps* understandably as Paine was so prolific later.

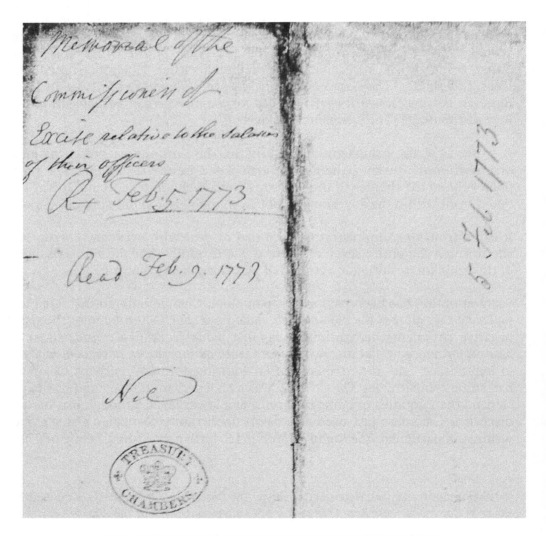

THE ANSWER FROM THE LORDS OF THE TREASURY 'NIL'

CHAPTER 8

George Lewis Scott, Thomas Paine and Benjamin Franklin

According to Hindmarch, Paine was George Lewis Scott's protégé. Below is a collection of notes and references that reveal the connections between Scott and Paine, first from Chalmers' *Life of Paine*:

> *'...our author's interest with the late George Lewis Scott, who had been appointed a commissioner of excise in 1758; and who having been at first captivated by the softness of his manner, which concealed the harshness of his spirit. When his patron, whose literature is remembered, while his benevolence is forgotten, could not, for the third time, obtain our author's restoration as an Officer of Excise, he recommended him strongly to that great man Dr Benjamin Franklin, as a person who could, at that epoch, be useful in America.'*[53]

It is not clear why Chalmers claimed that Scott could not restore Paine to the Excise Service for the *'third time.'* From the minute books Paine was only restored once, after his discharge from Alford. It may be that Paine appealed for restoration after his discharge from Lewes but no record has survived if so. Dr. Benjamin Franklin, at the time of Paine's introduction, was in the employ of the King as Postmaster General of the North American colonies. This was a critical stage in the development of the American insurgence, well reported in the Lewes Journal.

A letter from George Lewis Scott's widow, Sarah Scott, to her sister in 1792:

> *'I have not seen the pamphlet you mention, but hope I shall do so. Paine seems to have found out his proper niche, he is quite worthy to associate with such legislators. I have just been reading his life, having more curiosity in regard to him than he is worthy of exciting, from learning that he was a protégé of Mr Scott's which indeed I knew before, from having*

---

[53] Francis Oldys [George Chalmers], *The Life of Thomas Pain; The Author of Rights of Man with a Defence of His Writings* (3rd Edition, London, 1791), p. 29.

been applied to by the author [Chalmers] to furnish him with any anecdotes I might be acquainted with during their connexion, but I could give the enquirer no satisfaction, as their intercourse began not till some years after I left Mr Scott.'[54]

The references from Chalmers showed that he was detailed and assiduous in his research. He had sight of official records and followed these up with interviews of family members.

Paine's Letter to the Excise Office, Broad Street, London, 24 March 1774:

'Dear Sir
I have requested Mr. Scott to put ye 3rd and 4th ride books book for 74 under examination, for as I was in London almost all last winter, I have no other, which have any business in them. Request the favour (if not too inconvenient) to inquire and inform me when they are ordered, and if you can find out the examiner, desire you will drink a bottle or two of wine with him, I should like the character to go in as fair as it can.'[55]

Paine's letter to the head office is revealing; he invoked Scott's name in the first instance in directly requesting his assistance, showing that he had access to the most senior Commissioner. This was written well after his involvement with *The Case*, as the 'NIL' response from the Treasury to the petition was on 9 February 1773. Paine's final discharge from the Excise Service **was made on 8 April 1774**, soon after writing this letter. Paine clearly wanted to keep his job when he wrote the letter just a few days earlier. The campaign having failed, perhaps the Commissioners thought it prudent to distance themselves from agitation. The letter below was written to Henry Laurens after Paine had published *Common Sense* in America.

Paine's letter to Henry Laurens, 14 January 1779, from Philadelphia:

'...As I always had a taste to science, I naturally had friends of that cast in England; and among the rest George Lewis Scott, Esq., whose formal introduction my first acquaintance with Dr Franklin commenced. I esteem Mr. Scott as one of the most amiable characters I know of, but his particular situation had been that in the minority of the present King he was his sub preceptor, and from the occasional traditionary accounts yet remaining in the family of Mr. Scott, I obtained the true character of the present King from his childhood upwards, and you may naturally sup-

---

54 Sarah Scott to [her sister] Elizabeth Montagu (9 January [1792]), Henry E. Huntington Library, San Marino, California: MO 5483.

55 Francis Oldys [George Chalmers], *The Life of Thomas Pain; The Author of Rights of Man with a Defence of His Writings* (3rd Edition, London, 1791), p. 32.

pose, of the present ministry. I saw the people of this country were all wrong, by an ill-placed confidence.

I wrote to Mr. Scott in May 1775, by Captain James Josiah, now in this city. I read the letter to him before I closed it. I used it in this free expression: **"Surely the ministry are all mad; they will never be able to conquer America."'**[56]

This is the most telling letter with regard to Paine's relationship with Scott. It informs us of how close he must have been to Paine, as Scott had divulged sensitive material about the king and his ministry. It was the king's ministry that had rejected the campaign for higher pay, and it was this same ministry that was getting it wrong with America. Having colluded with Scott in trying to assist the king and his ministry, Paine here in full makes a free critical comment on how the administration just cannot see common sense, again. Paine and Scott must have decided together that it was hopeless trying to sort out the ministry with logic. They had tried that with the campaign for higher pay over a long time and in depth. Paine and Scott must have spent time together, not only plotting the campaign but also sharing confidences. Scott died on 7 December 1780 whilst still in post at the Excise. The letter that Paine sent to Scott indicated that they both would have agreed on a negative opinion of the king's ministry. The content would have been interpreted as seditious if not traitorous, and dangerous to Scott in the extreme.

Scott knew Dr. Benjamin Franklin well; they were fellow members of the Royal Society. At the time when Scott introduced Paine to Franklin, things were starting to heat up in the American colonies. The introduction of Paine to Franklin by Scott perhaps holds more intrigue than previously thought. Franklin openly criticised the ministry in a letter to the *Public Advertiser* in December 1773 about their plan to stop emigration to America.[57] There followed a public rebuke, perhaps tongue in cheek, from Brittanicus, an anonymous writer (perhaps Franklin himself) using a pseudonym: *'As it is settled Point in Government here, that every Man has his Price, 'tis plain they are Bunglers in their Business, and have not given him enough.'* Here the unknown author was making a comment about how good the British government had been to Franklin by awarding him with the rank of Postmaster General of America, making his son a governor, and also having offered him a post of £500 a year in the Salt Office if he would relinquish his ardour for America.[58]

---

[56] Thomas Paine, *The Complete Writings of Thomas Paine*, ed. Philip S. Foner, vol. 2 (New York, 1945), p. 1162.

[57] Benjamin Franklin, 'On a Proposed Act to Prevent Emigration' (December 1773), *The Papers of Benjamin Franklin*, ed. William B. Willcox, vol. 20, (New Haven, 1976), pp. 522-528.

[58] Brittanicus [pseudonym, author unknown], 'A letter to the Publick Advertiser' (before 31 January 1774), *The Papers of Benjamin Franklin*, ed. William B. Willcox, vol. 21 (New Haven, 1978), pp. 72-73.

Just days before Paine was discharged from Lewes, Franklin sent another open letter to the *Public Advertiser*, this time addressed directly to Lord North, **on 5 April 1774.** This was a witty attack on the parlous state of the ministry in their approach to the troublesome American Colonists. Franklin proposed that the British ministry introduce into America, without delay a government absolutely and entirely military: **'I humbly propose that the General and Commander in Chief be vested with the Power, and called by the Name of the King's Viceroy of all North America. This will serve to impress the Americans with greater Respect for the first Magistrate, and have a Tendency to secure their Submission.'[59]** To write such a letter in public was provocative in the extreme.

That letter turned out to be prescient. Franklins' letter of introduction for Thomas Paine set a train of events in motion that made his open letter to Lord North a reality. Franklins' letter to his son-in-law in London, 30 September 1774:

> *'Dear Son,*
>
> *The bearer, Mr. Thomas Paine, is very well recommended to me, as an ingenious, worthy young man. He goes to Pennsylvania with a view of settling there. I request you to give him your best advice and countenance, as he is quite a stranger there. If you can put him in a way of obtaining employment as a clerk, or assistant tutor in a school, or assistant surveyor, (of all which I think him very capable,) so that he may procure a subsistence at least, till he can make acquaintance and obtain a knowledge of the country, you will do well, and much oblige your affectionate father. My love to Sally and the boys.*
>
> *B. Franklin.'*

George Lewis Scott (1708-1780) was born in Hanover in May 1708, the elder son of James and Marion Scott of Bristol. Marion née Stewart was the daughter of the Lord Advocate in Scotland. James and Marion Scott made their way to Hanover to gain favour with the future royal family, and James was eventually appointed Envoy Extraordinary to the Polish-Saxon court and then minister to the court of Prussia. The heir to the English throne at that time, Dowager Electress Sophia, agreed to be the infant Scott's godmother, and he was named George Lewis after her eldest son. George Lewis Scott attended Leiden University in 1727 and was eventually called to the bar at the middle Temple in England on 3 June 1736. He also became a Fellow of the Society of Antiquaries on 3 June 1736, and was made a Fellow of the Royal Society on 5 May 1737, all in addition to being a founding member of the Society for the En-

---

[59] Benjamin Franklin, 'An Open Letter to Lord North' (5 April [printed in the newspaper 15 April] 1774), *The Papers of Benjamin Franklin*, ed. William B. Willcox, vol. 21 (New Haven, 1978), pp. 183-186.

couragement of Learning. Scott was on the Board of Longitude, which granted the prize to John Harrison for the first marine chronometer. He was a pupil of the brilliant mathematician de Moivre, was more than proficient on the harpsichord, and made a significant contribution to the selection, revision, and expansion of Ephraim Chambers's *Dictionary of Arts and Sciences,* for which he received £1500. Scott was extremely well connected and counted the great Samuel Johnson amongst his acquaintances.[60] Scott had matured fully by the time he was called to the bar in 1736; he clearly enmeshed fully with the highest levels of society and would have been well aware of the political situation of the day.

Scott was recommended by Lord Bolingbroke to the post of sub-preceptor (tutor) to Prince George, later to be crowned King George III. This was a controversial appointment, as Bolingbroke was a patriot Tory who vigorously attacked King George II's Whig ministry. He ridiculed Whig policies and corruption through nearly a hundred essays in *The Craftsman,* surgically exposing the iniquities of a Whig dynasty represented by the kings' chief minister, Robert Walpole. *The Craftsman,* a journalistic venture, was a large component of a formidable and sophisticated political campaign. From 1728 to 1732 it was published weekly. Up to 12,000 copies were distributed and reprinted in several provincial towns.[61]

There were accusations, due to the Bolingbroke recommendation, that Scott was a Jacobite, and believed in the divine right of kings, antithesis to the Hanoverian dynasty. No one took these charges seriously apart from the political opponents of Bolingbroke, led by Walpole. Scott defended himself in writing, laying out his plans of education for the young Prince George. He was supported by the Princess of Wales and taught the prince Latin, French, history, and geography until the prince's eighteenth birthday in June 1756. Due to political jockeying, Scott did not remain in the Prince's service as he had hoped, but he was able to resign, receiving a pension of £500 *'equivalent to my former salary...settled without any difficulty & without deduction, till some proper place offered.'* The prince let it be known through Lord Bute that a position in either the Customs or the Excise Service would be suitable for Scott's talents. Bute communicated this to the Duke of Devonshire, and then the Duke of Newcastle, successive First Lords of the Treasury. Newcastle was in post when a vacancy became available, and Bute renewed his recommendation of Scott. He was appointed onto the Board of Commissioners of the Excise Ser-

---

[60] W. P. Courtney, 'Scott, George Lewis (1708-1780), mathematician', *Oxford Dictionary of National Biography* (2011).

[61] H. T. Dickinson, 'St John, Henry, styled first Viscount Bolingbroke (1678-1751), politician, diplomatist, and author', *Oxford Dictionary of National Biography* (2013).

vice with a yearly salary of £1000 in February 1758.[62] Two years later, on 25 October 1760 at the age of 22, the young prince was crowned George III, King of Great Britain and Ireland.

Scott showed a strong interest in publishing and printed material as one of the founders of the Society for The Encouragement of Learning in 1735. The aim was to 'Assist authors in the publication, and to Secure to them the entire profits of their own Works.'[63] It was co-founded with the 2nd Duke of Richmond from Sussex and other eminent gentlemen of the day. The society was dissolved in 1749. Inspection of Memoirs of the Society for the Encouragement of Learning[64] showed a close working relationship between the Society and stationers of which James Bettenham was one. He was called to a meeting of the Society in 1737 at which Scott was present. William Lee was Bettenham's apprentice from 1729 for seven years and in his employ until 1744. In 1739 William Lee printed Benjamin Martin's The Description and Use of a New Invented Pocket Reflecting Microscope with a Micrometer. Lee started the first newspaper in Sussex, The Sussex Weekly Advertiser or Lewes Journal, in 1745.[65] Paine mentioned in The Age of Reason that he had attended Martin's lectures in one of his sojourns in London:

> 'The natural bent of my mind was to science. I had some turn, and I believe some talent, for poetry; but this I rather repressed than encouraged, as leading too much onto the field of imagination. As soon as I was able I purchased a pair of globes and attended the philosophical lectures of Martin and Ferguson, and became afterward acquainted with Dr. Bevis, of the society called the Royal Society, then living in the Temple, and an excellent astronomer.
>
> I had no disposition for what is called politics. It presented to my mind no other idea than as contained in the word Jockeyship. When, therefore, I turned my thoughts toward matter of government I had to form a system for myself that accorded with the moral and philosophical principles in which I had been educated.

---

[62] Barbara Brandon Schnorrenberg, 'Who Was George Lewis Scott?', New Perspectives on the Eighteenth Century, vol. 2 (2005), p. 46.

[63] Clayton Howard Atto, 'The Society for The Encouragement of Learning and its place in the history of publishing', Historical Research, vol. 17, no. 9 (June 1939), pp. 41-42.

[64] BL Add Mss 6191 6192.

[65] T. J. McCann, 'Eighteenth Century Printing in Chichester', Sussex Archaeological Collections, vol. 130 (1992), p. 190.

I saw, at least I thought I saw, a vast scene opening itself to the world in the affairs of America.[66]

Paine wrote the above in 1793. It is most likely that Paine attended these lectures in the early 1770's when Martin as well as James Ferguson were giving lectures in London at the same time.[67] Paine was in London regularly, collecting material to write *The Case*, as verified from the letter from Thomas Paine to Oliver Goldsmith dated 21 December 1772, written from the Excise Coffee House in Broad Street. By 1772, Paine had achieved a higher status, having been chosen to write *The Case*, and thus it was more likely that he would be introduced to people of standing. Paine mentioned Bevis, a member of the Royal Society, as were Scott, Franklin, and Ferguson. Lee, who printed *The Case*, had printed Martin's book earlier.

Paine's reference to his talent in writing poetry was not unfounded; he wrote *Farmer Short's dog Porter: A Tale* in Lewes, a satire on the stupidity of the local magistrates after a farmer had made the mistake of voting for the wrong parliamentary candidate. Paine subsequently published this poem in the *Pennsylvania Magazine* in July 1775.[68] The concepts of politics as 'Jockeyship' and America as 'a vast scene opening itself to the world' could have been introduced to him by his acquaintance with Scott and Franklin, but also by what he had read weekly for the last six years in *The Sussex Weekly Advertiser or Lewes Journal*. Paine had a rare insight into the dysfunction of government, laid bare in *The Case*. This insight was enabled by George Lewis Scott. Working closely with the man at the top would have been a rare insight for an ordinary officer. It was this one factor that was most important in Paine's development. The proximity to real power must have been breathtaking and confidence-building at the same time. Franklin wrote publicly about the ministry getting it wrong regarding America. It is the contention of the next chapter to show that what he read every week in his local newspaper, owned and composited by Lee, reinforced his view that the ministry was awry: not just economically in refusing higher pay, but in all the major issues of the day whether at home or abroad.

---

[66] Thomas Paine, *The Complete Writings of Thomas Paine*, ed. Philip S. Foner, vol. 1 (New York, 1945), p. 496.

[67] J. R. Millburn, 'The London evening courses of Benjamin Martin and James Ferguson, eighteenth-century lecturers on experimental philosophy', *Annals of Science*, vol. 40, no. 5 (1983), pp. 437-455.

[68] W. A. Speck, *A Political Biography of Thomas Paine* (London, 2013), p. 17.

CHAPTER 9

The Sussex Weekly Advertiser or Lewes Journal

To trawl through this newspaper is exciting and revealing. Breaking news from the 18c, details abound of individuals, incidents, and dramas written in an uninhibited style. The themes and storylines considered to have been of interest to Paine were of a political nature. In this case, the details that would have been of interest to Paine are of such quantity that a systematic approach had to be developed. The first search was made on the microfiche files that are held in the Lewes library. It has been known for some time that Elizabeth Paine, his wife, and Samuel Ollive, his father-in-law, were mentioned in short articles about Ollive's death, later about Elizabeth and Paine setting up shop, and later still the sale of the assets of the shop. Whilst looking on the microfiche for Paine-related material I noticed that **William Lee, the owner and editor, reprinted some of the letters of Junius, whose identity remains a mystery to this day.** Junius attacked leading ministers from 1769-1772 with letters published in the London newspaper, the *Public Advertiser*, owned and printed by Henry Sampson Woodfall.

Junius wrote about issues surrounding John Wilkes, Corsica, and America, along with accurate and damning details about the corruption of individual ministers. The Wilkes affair raged through these years. The dispute was caused by the fact that although he polled the most votes in the Middlesex election, Parliament would not let Wilkes take his seat, instead choosing Col. Luttrell, the ministers' favourite candidate. Junius and the country saw that the freedoms and liberty of the country were under threat; there were riots which provided long-running storylines in the newspaper. In addition to this, it was perceived that the ministry was getting its policy on Corsica wrong by not supporting General Paoli in resisting the French. Moreover, the North American colonists were held up as a bastion of freedom who were being taxed and treated unfairly by Parliament.

In order to read the newspapers better, with the cooperation of the East Sussex Library Service, in particular Michelle Brooker, we sent the microfiche off to Microstat to be scanned into PDF files. The copy is, to use technical terms, too dirty and smudgy to apply a text conversion software to it, so it could not be rendered word-searchable. Even so, the high-resolution PDF files have made the editions of the newspaper much easier to read. The first task was to classify the years, months, and weeks of the pdf images; the material that we scanned are some editions from 1762-1769 and every edition from 1769-1776. Because the editions are not word-searchable, every article in every edition has had to be read to ascertain its content. This was a huge task and is still a work in progress. These editions of the Sussex Weekly Advertiser or Lewes Journal warrant a study of their own, with perhaps many articles and books that could be written on the content.

This newspaper is a rich resource; Paine would have read this carefully whilst he was in Lewes. Colin Brent claimed convincingly that Paine wrote two letters that were published in the newspaper, one showing the unfairness of the Poor Law in England at that time, the second a design for a fire escape.[69] Especially considering the fact that the owner of the newspaper, William Lee, printed *The Case*, Paine would surely have paid close attention to what was contained in the newspaper. The *Sussex Weekly Advertiser* was the main easily available source of information, covering international, national, and local news. Peter Chasseaud is the expert on the way the newspaper was printed; for the type of press and the type of paper used, see Appendix Three.

Now that the editions can be seen in high resolution on a large screen, they are much easier to read. With the PDF files it has been possible to zoom in and really access the text. It has also been possible to annotate duplicate copies of the editions; in this way, the topics have been colour coded. At the same time, a word document has been set up for every edition, with a short description of every article of interest, a classification allowing a speedy way back to the original article using a key word and a colour to assist visualisation.

Being able to see it like this made it easier to see how Lee composed the paper. The *Lewes Journal* was a weekly newspaper, with each new edition issued on Mondays. There was very little news about Lewes or Sussex. What there was appeared on page four, often covering half the page, which was then finished with advertisements. Local news was scant; what dominated the newspaper was international news and national stories. Lee followed the convention for provincial newspapers of the mid-18c of copying, day by day, what was published in the London newspapers. This resulted in the conflation of any given storyline. Lee received London newspapers every day and reprinted their news reports under various headings including *'Foreign Intelligence'* and *'Mail from Flanders'*. The London newspapers were mostly not identified, but collected under a subtitle, *'London,'* with the date alongside. This repeated

---

[69] Colin Brent, 'Thirty Something: Thomas Paine at Bull House in Lewes, 1768-74 - Six Formative Years', *Sussex Archaeological Society Collections,* vol. 147 (2009), pp. 153-67.

through the edition day by day with the occasional insert of a heading, 'Country News,' which contained reports from other cities and counties. Now and again a title of the London newspaper was mentioned, but not often. The *Public Advertiser* was mentioned more than any other. 'American News' appeared as a heading on its own. *The London Gazette,* the king's newspaper, was nearly always identified; the information in these articles was very pro-ministry and contained announcements of the king and his court gatherings, known as levees. By the middle of the 18c, there were 18 newspapers printed in London: six weeklies, six tri-weeklies, and six dailies.[70]

The two political camps of the 18c were Whigs and Tories, and it was common in the mid-18c for provincial newspaper owners to appeal to both alike.[71] Clio Rickman, a fellow Lewesian and lifelong friend, claimed that Paine was a Whig during his time in Lewes.[72] Professor Bill Speck noted that the term Whig entered the political vocabulary in England in the 1680's to counter the Tory claim that kings ruled by divine right. This was settled in the Glorious Revolution of 1688, where the balance of power was set up more or less equitably between the House of Commons, the House of Lords, and the Crown, dispensing with the idea of the divine right to rule.[73] By the time Paine was old enough to be aware of politics there were two kinds of Whigs: the Country Whigs, upholding the sovereignty of the people, some to the point of republicanism, and the Court Whigs, asserting that sovereign power lay with the king in Parliament.

George III defeated the Whig oligarchy fairly soon after he was crowned; in just six years he achieved the fall of the Whig-dominated ministry. The new king was determined to regain for the monarchy the influence lost during the reigns of the first two Hanoverian monarchs. He perceived that the narrow Whig oligarchy had taken advantage of a disputed succession and a foreign ruling family to control the state. This much can be seen in the oaths that the Excise men had to swear. King George II had declared, *'ministers were kings in this country.'*[74] The young king, by the time Paine had settled in Lewes, had appointed his own men to high ministerial office. Junius attacked the ministry, and the Whig press followed.

---

[70] Hannah Barker, *Newspapers, Politics and English Society, 1695-1855* (London, 2000), p. 29.

[71] G. A. Cranfield, *The Development of the Provincial Newspaper, 1700-1760* (Oxford, 1962), p. 117.

[72] T. Clio Rickman, *The Life of Thomas Paine* (London, 1819), p. 17.

[73] This information was conveyed to Paul Myles by William Speck on the occasion of a public event in the House of Commons welcoming Norman Baker MP as president of The Thomas Paine Society for a two-year term in 2013. Norman was a Home Office minister at the time. The talk was given by Paul Myles on the topic of the history of the idea of Liberalism.

[74] D. A. Winstanley, *Lord Chatham and the Whig Opposition* (London, 1966), p. 2.

It is the purpose of this chapter to show what Paine would have seen, and how it was reported, in the *Lewes Journal*. Without going into minute detail regarding the whole political landscape, by just looking at the sheer weight of the anti-ministry rhetoric in the column inches it can be seen how Paine was influenced. Paine had the inside story of how inept the ministry and the Lords of the Treasury were in not recognising the parlous state of the Excise Collection. He could also see that ineptitude when dealing with other important matters of state in the press. The inventive way that the reporting took place is astonishing. The writing was often very good. The storylines were reported as they moved forward, day by day and week by week, with many repeats in the same day due to any story being reported in a slightly different way by the different London newspapers. This resulted in one storyline being repeated many times under any one day's reporting from London. This provided an iteration of a news article, not dissimilar to the social media exposure of 2018. The repeats of a 'meme,' an idea, was remarkable. One could read the same reporting on one instance perhaps twenty times on the same page. It would be impossible to assess the effect that this would have on a reader, but an important factor is that in Sussex there would have been no competition for the reader's attention. There was no other media in competition. If the reader saw one of the London newspapers the stories would be roughly the same, as the provincial papers copied those articles.

There is too much information contained in the Lewes newspaper to cover all the storylines that gripped the nation through these turbulent years. There was such turmoil over the John Wilkes issue that it forced the government to accept parliamentary reporting in newspapers fully for the first time. Until this period, there was a prohibition of parliamentary reporting in place; loopholes had been exploited by magazines but these were closed by a resolution of the House of Commons on 13 April 1738.

1769 through to 1774 was the hot period in which Paine would have witnessed these issues being fought out in the Lewes newspaper. That of parliamentary reporting was the most boldly reported; John Almon claimed the breakthrough moment in his memoir:

> 'When the spirit of the nation was raised high by the massacre in St George's fields, the unjust decision upon the Middlesex election, etc, Mr Almon resolved the nation acquainted with the proceedings of Parliament: for this purpose he employed himself sedulously in obtaining from different gentlemen......sufficient to write a sketch of every days debate, on the most important and interesting questions, which he printed three times a week regularly in the London Evening Post...'

The massacre that was referred to was the suppression of a riot outside King's Bench Prison, where Wilkes was confined, on 10 May 1768. Five people were killed by soldiers in maintaining order.[75]

The rise of the provincial newspapers, along with parliamentary reporting, allowed for the first time in a very turbulent period a whole new vocabulary of politics. During this period, the newspapers changed from being a mere vehicle of news to becoming a political weapon. It is in this period that we see the origins of the parliamentary sketch writer, leading to newspapers being used to shape opinion. This was not peculiar to Lewes, but it had more importance there, where this explosion of opinion and political rancour acted upon Thomas Paine's mind, which had been prepared by his experience in the Excise Service. It is not the argument here that William Lee was particularly biased in favour of the Tories or the Whigs. There are more pro-Whig articles in the newspaper and certainly a lot more anti-ministry articles, but that is more than likely a reflection of what was printed in the London press from which he drew. It is hard to assess, for very little is known about William Lee. Lee selected what articles were recomposited into the newspaper, but this was not a simple matter of cut and paste; as a businessman, he would have wanted to avoid expensive prosecution for libel or worse from the Crowns' agents. He also would not have wanted to alienate one side or another from buying his newspaper.

The main storylines of Wilkes, America, and Corsica

Before we show the frequency of, and the emphasis that was placed on, these three main storylines, a brief description of each will set the mid-18c scene.

Wilkes

Wilkes had fallen foul of the king and his ministry; when he was a sitting MP he criticised Lord Bute, King George III's favourite minister, in his political weekly the *North Briton*, issue no. 45, on 23 April 1763. Wilkes was imprisoned for a short time in the Tower of London and charged with sedition. He was released on a technicality; his arrest was made under a *'general warrant,'* which did not stand in court. During his defence the cry first went up *'Wilkes and Liberty!'* This slogan endured and resounded until 1774 all over the United Kingdom and the North American colonies. Wilkes came to represent everything that was rotten with the king and his ministry. The ancient freedoms hard fought for over the centuries were perceived to be under very real threat. Magna Carta was invoked, and the Bill of Rights and the Glorious Revolution were constantly referred to in the press. Matters became even worse.

---

[75] Peter D. G. Thomas, 'The Beginning of Parliamentary Reporting in Newspapers, 1768-1774', *The English Historical Review*, vol. 74, no. 293 (October 1959), pp. 623-636.

Wilkes left the country after he was challenged to a duel by Samuel Martin MP and received a grievous wound. To avoid further prosecution Wilkes retired to Paris and was outlawed in November 1764, having been expelled from the House of Commons.

Wilkes remained abroad for four years, as his return would have meant imprisonment. He liquidated his assets in England but never received most of the money due to the dishonest handling of these transactions by his friend, Humphrey Cotes. Finding himself unable to obtain a pardon, Wilkes decided to return, and intended to obtain a parliamentary seat. He failed to be elected in the City of London, and promptly announced he would contest the Middlesex seat on 28 March 1768, and he was successful. Right up until this moment the threat of imprisonment had hung over him from the eventually successful 1764 prosecutions of his having written a salacious article, the *Essay on Woman*, and for publishing the *North Briton*. He had not been apprehended, but was expelled from Parliament again in anticipation of his court appearance on 20 April 1768.

Wilkes delivered himself into King's Bench Prison, and remained there until March 1770, being elected to and expelled from Parliament again. Wilkes was elected once more, but Parliament declared his opponent, Henry Luttrel, the winner although he polled only 296 votes against Wilkes's 1143. Wilkes secured election as Alderman for the Ward of Farringdon Without in January 1769, and the **Society of Gentlemen Supporters of the Bill of Rights** was formed to raise funds for Wilkes, who would have remained in King's Bench Prison if he could not have discharged his debts, estimated at £14,000. A split amongst Wilkesites led to another society being formed, the **Constitutional Society,** but both groups worked together in a simultaneous contest with the House of Commons over parliamentary reporting.[76] These concerted efforts also led to petitions being made directly to King George from electors all over the country, first from the Middlesex electors and then from all over the nation, including the London Livery. It was estimated that between a quarter and a third of England's voters signed one of these petitions during 1769 and early 1770.[77] The number of petitions, details of where they came from, the petitions in full, how they were presented to the king, and how they were received were reported daily in the *Lewes Journal* in abundance. Paine was, during these formative years, setting up the campaign for higher pay for the Excise Officers. Petitions, as we have seen, were presented in 1769 by the officers of Wales and Hereford to the Lords of the Treasury for higher pay. Americans noted that *'private letters from almost every county in England that*

---

[76] Peter D. G. Thomas, 'Wilkes, John (1725-1797), politician', *Oxford Dictionary of National Biography* (2008).

[77] Pauline Maier, 'John Wilkes and American Disillusionment with Britain', *The William and Mary Quarterly*, vol. 20, no. 3 (July 1963), p. 390.

there is no other language to be heard, from highest to lowest, but **petition, petition, petition!'**[78]

America

Whilst Wilkes was the focus of most attention in the early years of 1769-1774, the American issue gained momentum over the six years Paine was in Lewes. America was well reported in the *Lewes Journal,* and the topic had its own title. The Sussex public was very well informed about the growing tension in the North American colonies via the pages in the newspaper. As the Wilkes furore faded in the early 1770's the American insurgence gathered pace. The American colonies were already sensitised to misuse by the British ministry by the Grenville Stamp Act, applied to the American colonies in 1765. This was a levy imposed on legal papers and other documents. Earlier colonial reforms in 1764 by Grenville had consisted of imposing new officials, judges, and customs officers to ensure America paid its share of the upkeep of British forces, including the navy. Grenville, who was the First Lord of the Treasury, and his fellow ministers were attempting to repeat the strategy that had been in place in Ireland since before 1720. Ireland was a conquered dominion where, despite having their own way of doing things, people knew where the ultimate authority lay. In 1720, Parliament passed a statute, the Declaratory Act, which encapsulated the situation: when the need arose, the British could make whatever law they chose for the Irish. The conquered nation effectively had to pay for the standing army that kept it in control.[79]

This strategy was difficult to enact in Ireland, and America was much further away. From Boston down to Georgia the North American colonists resisted what they saw as unfair British control. Grenville fell from power at the end of 1765, and the Stamp Act was repealed by the new Whig administration. The American slogan, **'no taxation without representation,'** was a common cry of the colonists. Another Declaratory Act was passed by the British government in early 1766, which insisted that Parliament was sovereign in every corner of the North American colonies, similar to Ireland. As well as inflaming the American colonists, it also opened a chasm between the competing views in the United Kingdom. The Rockingham Whig ministry fell in July 1766, which marked a profound change for George III; he had at last removed the Whig oligarchy which had reduced the previous two Hanoverian kings' power to run their own ministry.[80] The Tories were now in control, and the Chancellor of the Exchequer, Charles Townshend, imposed another round of taxes on

---

[78] Pauline Maier, 'John Wilkes and American Disillusionment with Britain', *The William and Mary Quarterly,* vol. 20, no. 3 (July 1963), p. 390.

[79] Nick Bunker, *An Empire on the Edge: How Britain came to Fight America* (London, 2015), p. 20.

[80] D. A. Winstanley, *Lord Chatham and the Whig Opposition* (London, 1966), p. 110.

North America, known as the Townshend duties. The new taxes were levied on a list of articles, including glass, paint, lead, paper, and tea. This caused a new storm of protest and a boycott of trade with the United Kingdom, the results of which set up North America to respond strongly to what was to come. Lord North repealed the Townshend duties in 1770 except for one, the duty on tea. These storylines were very well reported in the *Lewes Journal*, and the reporting was clear and concise. Thomas Paine was well informed regarding the North American agitation without having to have any special connections or intelligence; he could simply read his local newspaper.

Wilkes and America

There was an interaction between the Wilkes affair and the American insurgence. The North American colonists picked up strongly on the Wilkesite cause, tracking every move from its inception in 1763. The Wilkesite call of *'Wilkes and Liberty'* resounded in America every bit as strongly as in England, if not more as they were also suffering from what they saw as unfair taxation and an arrogant attitude of overlordship on the part of the British ministry. Gifts were sent from America to Wilkes, some exotic; a turtle was sent to Wilkes weighing 45 pounds, 45 being the number of the edition of the *North Briton* for which Wilkes was originally arrested. 45 candles were lit on a liberty tree and 45 bowls of punch were laid at a banquet in Wilkes's honour.[81] As early as 1763 merchants of major ports in America formed committees in order to remonstrate against the taxes imposed by the British ministry, suspending British imports. The American presses operated much the same way as in England, with Boston as the centre of the press reports. Articles originating in Boston were repeated throughout the colonies, similar to the provincial newspapers in England repeating the London papers.[82] Moreover, reports from American newspapers came back to England, were repeated in the London press and then proliferated through the provincial papers of England.

Corsica

Although the Corsican issue was not as much of a cause célèbre as Wilkes and America, it is mentioned here since Junius referred to it as another thing that the ministry had misjudged. There was infighting within the ministry. General Paoli had asked for assistance from England to resist the threat from France. Lord Shelburne, the Secretary of State for the Southern Department, was strongly in favour of providing assistance to Paoli in order to prevent the French from getting a foothold on the island. He was overruled by the Tory faction, who viewed Shelburne with suspicion and at that time did not want to

---

[81] Pauline Maier, 'John Wilkes and American Disillusionment with Britain', *The William and Mary Quarterly*, vol. 20, no. 3 (July 1963), p. 379.

[82] Arthur M. Schlesinger, *Prelude to Independence: The Newspaper War on Britain 1764-1776* (New York, 1958), p. 91.

increase tensions with France. In addition to this stance on Corsican issues Shelburne had already declared that he felt the taxes imposed on America were illegal. As a result of these two major differences between him and those in power, Shelburne was removed from the ministry in 1768. This was well reported in the press leading to the Corsican issue being generally viewed as another bungling by a corrupt ministry. References to General Paoli in the papers joined the Wilkesite and American causes of liberty.

The editions of The Sussex Weekly Advertiser or Lewes Journal for the twelve months of 1769

The number of articles on each of the main topics for the 51 editions of the whole year of 1769 were:

Wilkes	799
Corsica	143
King & Ministry	197
America	70
Junius	18

Although the count is useful to get an initial feel, not all articles are equal. They differ in length, from a very short insert to a whole page. Column inches could be a measure, but the articles also vary in novelty, semantic punch, and humour. The articles range from the profound to the ridiculous. Very often the humorous articles on a serious subject are an entertainment in themselves.

THE SUSSEX WEEKLY ADVERTISER OR LEWES JOURNAL

CHAPTER 10

Conclusion

This study is an attempt to consider Thomas Paine in context: his experience in the Excise Service, his coming of age in the independently-minded, dissenting county town of Lewes, his exposure to and relationship with a lively provincial newspaper, and his contact with operators at the highest level on the London scene have all been examined. These immediate life experiences would have acted most strongly on his mind. The proximal argument is made here, that the objects that he saw every day, events that threatened his livelihood, and connections promising promotion would have mattered more than any theoretical assumptions. The new information about the signatures of the Excise men from Wales, the more detailed look at the rooting out of corruption in the Cornwall Collection, evidence that Paine was subject to unfair treatment himself in the service, and a much more detailed look at the *Lewes Journal*: these accounts, drawn together for the first time, explain how Paine was able to write *The Case* with conviction.

The Case represents, for the first time, an attempt at a *national* campaign for better pay and working conditions. The first national unionisation of ordinary men in the largest group of government workers that collected revenue for the nation. Perhaps it is because they were Excise men, and that it was organised from close to the very heart of government, that this extraordinary fact has been hiding in plain sight for so many years.

We should celebrate that it was made in England, by a group of caring and responsible government workers, articulated by a very promising writer, the Englishman, Thomas Paine; a world first, ahead of its time. It is now time to acknowledge this achievement as a milestone in humanity. And perhaps look again at the underlying factors that brought *The Case* into being.

The final minute book entry with regard to Thomas Paine in the Excise Service, entered on 8 April 1774:

> *'Thomas Paine officer of Lewes 4th Out Ride Sussex Collection, having quitted his Business without obtaining the Boards Leave, for so doing, & being gone off on account of the Debts which he hath contracted, as by*

Letter of the 6th Inst. from Edward Clifford Supervisor, and the **said Paine having been once before Discharged; ORDERED that he be again Discharged.'**[83]

Paine's eventual discharge from the service in Lewes was odd. A substituting officer, Edward Clifford, was temporarily sent to Lewes. Clifford lodged a complaint that Paine was absent without leave. The message was rushed to London in an unseemly manner on 6 April 1774 in Lewes. The board's decision in London to discharge Paine was made on 8 April 1774. This clearly circumvented due process. The local Collector, the highest Excise official in Lewes, would normally have dealt with such an issue in the first instance.[84] Also, contrary to many claims made ever since, Paine did not go bankrupt; in fact, he was granted £45, a year's salary after deductions, in the separation settlement from his wife Elizabeth Paine. The business that he was on was directed by one of the Commissioners of Excise, George Lewis Scott, in the writing of *The Case*. The entry in the minute book was never seen by Paine. It was perhaps a discreet exercise to tidy up what might have been difficult to explain: that Paine was instructed to lead an attempt for the whole of the Excise Service.

Paine, along with Scott and many in the Excise Service, was attempting to improve the system from within the Excise Service. In this effort, it was necessary to understand the status quo, the inherent corruption. This corruption was amplified through the pages of *The Sussex Weekly Advertiser or Lewes Journal*. Whilst remaining loyal servants, Paine and Scott were critical of the existing system. The ability to operate in a loyal way whilst addressing the iniquities of a rotten, class-ridden system was present in them both. The final demonstration of this flexibility was shown in Paine's later letter to Scott, written in very familiar terms, notwithstanding the fact that Scott did not protect Paine from being discharged in the final act of the minute book.

This early writing by Thomas Paine clearly showed his humanity, his support for those who were not of the ruling class. His moral compass was set early in his life, exposed to the humanity of the Quaker faith by his father. Paine saw the iniquities of a rotten borough in his home town of Thetford, along with the advantages of belonging to the established church; his Anglican Mother arranged his entry into the Excise Service. It can be seen from the story told above that Thomas Paine formed his views and opinions from his experience in the Excise Service by operating at both the lowest and the highest levels. This was a rare insight, which, combined with a natural ability to write, resulted in a long and illustrious writing career. The ideas that flowed from Thomas Paine's pen did change the world, and still have the power to do so

---

[83] TNA: PRO, CUST 47/293, p. 21.

[84] George Hindmarch, 'Thomas Paine: The First Excise Period' (two versions, unpublished, East Sussex Records Offices, The Keep, ACC 10140/2).

again. The core principles that were expounded in *The Case* are fundamental to human nature. The principle of exposing corruption and providing a framework to overcome it is a requirement in any age, as needed today as it was in 1771.

Perhaps one of the most important agents for change in England and Wales was the very document that Paine wrote in support of his fellow Officers of Excise. *The Case* was distributed throughout the kingdom to every officer, and his argument was articulated clearly. They would have recognised every point that he made, and even though they did not get immediate action, over the next 50 years every one of Thomas Paine's recommendations was adopted.

FINIS.

©Penelope Parker

Analysis of The Case

Paine organised the pamphlet into four sections:

1. *The Introduction*

2. *The State of the Salary of the Officers of Excise*

3. *Thoughts on the Corruptions of Principles and on the numerous Evils arising to the Revenue from the too great Poverty of the Officers of Excise*

4. *Remarks on the Qualifications of Officers.*

The Introduction:

The purpose of *The Case* was made clear immediately, that it was *'not only expedient, but highly necessary to present a state of their case, previous to the presentation of their petition.'*

Paine argued that some cases were so reasonable *'that the more they are considered, the more weight they obtain.'* Reason, not demand, would encourage the reader to really think about what was to follow. He laid out that the forthcoming appeal would show that there would be nothing underhand about the claim; in fact, it was an example *'both of simplicity, and honest confidence'* of relief being granted immediately *'on having their case fully and perfectly known and understood.'*

Despite the simplicity of a singular request for higher pay for the Officers of Excise there was a complexity of why this had come about:

> *'It is a subject interwoven with a variety of reasons from different causes.'* The main thrust of the arguments to follow were laid out: *'If the poverty of the Officers of Excise; if the temptations arising from their poverty; if the qualifications of persons to be admitted into the employ-*

ment; if the security of the revenue itself, are matters of any weight, then I am conscious that my voluntary services in this business, will produce some good effect or other, either to the better security of the revenue, the relief of the officers, or both.'[85]

Paine laid out the themes that he was to expand upon whilst noting that he acted as a volunteer in this business. He wrote in his letter to Goldsmith that he was the *'Principal Promoter of a Plan for applying to Parliament this session for an increase of Salary.'* It is hard to imagine that Paine was the architect of the earlier petitions to the Lords of the Treasury. This would mean that he would have risen from the status of a discharged officer to running a national campaign, which must have been in the planning well before those petitions were presented in 1769. During that time, Paine was being offered posts in Grampound and Wells. It is more likely that Paine was chosen to write *The Case* after the national campaign had already been set up. Paine could have indicated that he was a volunteer for two reasons: firstly, that he did not receive payment for writing *The Case* but was allowed the time to write it on his salary as an Officer of Excise, and secondly, to protect the anonymity of the Commissioners of Excise and other officers above him.

The State of the Salary of the Officers of Excise

Paine showed a prose technique in *The Case* that became his hallmark throughout his long writing career, that of using striking comparisons for effect: on the one hand this and on the other hand that. The reader is led gently into this device at the beginning of this section. He also recruited the reader's senses, rather than just stating bald facts and figures. It began:

> *'When a year's salary is mentioned in the gross, it acquires a degree of consequence from its sound, which it would not have if separated into daily payments.... fifty pounds a year, and one shilling and nine-pence farthing a day, carry as different degrees of significancy with them, as my Lord's steward, and the steward's labourer; and yet an Out-Ride Officer in the Excise, under the name of fifty pounds a year receives for himself no more than one shilling and nine-pence farthing a day.'*[86]

The sound of a larger sum to the ear compared with the fact of a much reduced daily sum. The comparison of the high status of *'my Lord's steward'* with the low status of the steward's labourer was used to highlight the difference. Paine in fact had a Lord and a Lord's steward in Lewes. It was further explained that tax, sitting expenses, and the expenses of horse-keeping, not including *'the purchase at first, and the hazard of life,'* reduced £50 to £32. It is

---

[85] Thomas Paine, *The Case of the Officers of Excise* (Lewes, 1772), pp. iii-iv.

[86] Thomas Paine, *The Case of the Officers of Excise* (Lewes, 1772), p. 5.

this lower figure which divided by 365 days arrived at one shilling and nine-pence farthing a day. These descriptive juxtapositions marked Paine out as a very different writer to those who wrote the earlier petitions.

A description of the different types of Excise officer followed. *The Case* referred to out rides in the main as they were '*by far the most numerous,*' the proportion to the foot-walks being '*as eight is to five.*' The burden on all types of officers was the same but for different reasons. The out rides suffered the cost of horses and of being removed from their home county, whereas the foot-walks in town suffered higher rents and also removes, with the officers in the city of London suffering even higher living costs than all the others.

A particularly powerful passage described the inflationary times:

> '*If the increase of money in the kingdom is one cause of the high price of provisions, the case of the Excise Officers is peculiarly pitiable. No increase comes to them—They are shut out from the general blessing—They behold it like a map of Peru.*'[87]

Even Chalmers was impressed by Paine's writing in this passage, quoting the above line in his *Life of Pain*. Chalmers expanded that the Excise Officers' pay had always been little and was now made less by the rise in the price of provisions, the establishment of taxes, and the expansion of luxury, a derogatory term at that time.[88] Chalmers, writing for the state in order to defame Paine, was given access to official records. He also noted that there was a financial contribution to *The Case* by every Officer of Excise, which must have been on record when he looked in the early 1790's. He would not have had access to Paine's letter to Goldsmith at that time.

Paine pointed out that the '*wealthy and humane*' would not like the idea that their affluence should become the misfortune of others. His humanitarian values started to show in this sentence, introducing empathy as a factor; he was commenting on human nature. The next point showed a grasp of economics: '*Were the money in the kingdom to be increased double, the salary would in value be reduced one half. Every step upwards, is a step downwards with them.*'[89] This line suggests an input from someone who had a grasp of national

---

[87] Thomas Paine, *The Case of the Officers of Excise* (Lewes, 1772), pp. 6-7.

[88] Francis Oldys [George Chalmers], *The Life of Thomas Pain; The Author of Rights of Man with a Defence of His Writings* (3rd Edition, London, 1791), p. 28.

[89] Thomas Paine, *The Case of the Officers of Excise* (Lewes, 1772), p. 7

economics: Commissioner George Lewis Scott worked with fellow senior mathematicians in assessing national statistics.[90]

The theme of the Excise Officers being economically manacled continued by comparing their plight with that of a common labourer who could raise their rate, whereas the officers' pay was fixed. Also peculiar to the Officers of Excise was the fact that they were told where they had to work:

> 'as the law of their office removes them far from all their natural friends and relations, it consequently prevents those occasional assistances from them, which are serviceably felt in a family, and which even the poorest, amongst the poor enjoys.'[91]

Paine aligned the Excise Officers with the poor, finessing the point by describing the little things that could give relief when he wrote that Excise Officers were among those 'who, either out of benevolence, or pride, keep their children from nakedness, supply them occasionally with perhaps half a hog, a load of wood, a chaldron of coal,' further noting that this relief was often considered necessary for those poor who actually earned more daily than those in the Excise.

It is rare to find in any of Paine's writing any reference to his own personal life. The next passage described how Paine had helped a fellow officer, who with his young family was under orders to be removed. Paine loaned him a small sum, saving the officer from defaulting on his creditors, which would have compelled him to 'desert the duty of his office'. The officer repaid Paine and continued to manage 'as well as the narrowness of such circumstances can admit of.'

The workload of those in the Excise Service was then described as the most arduous under his Majesty's employment: 'The station may rather be called a seat of constant work, than either a place, or an employment.' This was in comparison with a riding officer's place in the customs, whose salary was £60 a year with an easier workload, and moreover:

> 'the work in the window-light duty, compared with the Excise, is lightness itself, yet their salary is subject to no tax, they receive forty-nine pounds twelve shillings and sixpence, without deduction.'[92]

---

[90] William Brakenridge, 'A Letter to George Lewis Scott, Esq.; F.R.S. concerning the number of people in England', *Philosophical Transactions of the Royal Society*, vol. 49 (1755-1756), pp. 268-285.

[91] Thomas Paine, *The Case of the Officers of Excise* (Lewes, 1772), p. 7.

[92] Thomas Paine, *The Case of the Officers of Excise* (Lewes, 1772), p. 8.

As mentioned earlier, personal comments or even references to Paine's own life, either by himself or those that were close to him, are very rare. Whilst Paine was making the point about low pay he mentioned celibacy. During his time in Lewes his marriage to Elizabeth Ollive was not consummated.[93] Elizabeth, Paine's young wife, must have invoked the canon law that was in force at that time, that was if the husband was incapable of consummating the marriage then the marriage was void. The wife could insist on an examination. Chalmers noted that a Dr. Manning reported *'apparent ability. Our Author said himself, "that he married for prudential reasons and abstained for prudential reasons."'*[94] Paine wrote in *The Case*:

> *'A single man may barely live; but as it is not the design of the Legislature, or the Honourable Board of Excise, to impose a state of celibacy on them, the condition of much the greater part is truly wretched and pitiable.'*[95]

The final part of this section set up the argument that by the time an Officer of Excise had realised that the pay was too low to subsist themselves, let alone a family, it was too late. The admission into Excise was fixed between 21 and 31 years old, a critically useful period of life. Therefore, the time spent learning the craft of gauging was time lost for learning a more profitable occupation. By the time the poor officer had realised this, there was no time left to learn a new trade. The skills that had been learnt in the Excise were often not required in the general workplace. *'Every year's experience gained in the Excise, is a year's experience lost in trade; and by the time they become wise officers, they become foolish workmen.'*[96] Very few Officers of Excise could gain promotion due to the structure of the service; a great number of ordinary officers were required to collect the revenue compared to the number of Supervisors and Collectors. It had already been recommended to members of the House of Commons by gentlemen and numbers of traders of opulence and reputation that injury was being done by the poverty of officers leading to fraud. Paine posed that *'the first is truly the case of the officers, but this is rather the case of the revenue,'*[97] showing that everyone was suffering: the honest trader, the Officers of Excise and, by damaging the revenue, the nation as a whole.

---

[93] Francis Oldys [George Chalmers], *The Life of Thomas Pain; The Author of Rights of Man with a Defence of His Writings* (3rd Edition, London, 1791), pp. 33-34.

[94] Francis Oldys [George Chalmers], *The Life of Thomas Pain; The Author of Rights of Man with a Defence of His Writings* (3rd Edition, London, 1791), p. 34.

[95] Thomas Paine, *The Case of the Officers of Excise* (Lewes, 1772), p. 9.

[96] Thomas Paine, *The Case of the Officers of Excise* (Lewes, 1772), p. 10.

[97] Thomas Paine, *The Case of the Officers of Excise* (Lewes, 1772), p. 10.

Thoughts on the Corruptions of Principles and on the numerous Evils arising to the Revenue from the too great Poverty of the Officers of Excise

Trust is the major theme of this section. Paine claimed that the wisdom of government had in many instances awarded large salaries in proportion to the position of trust to set men above temptation. For example, the large salaries of judges made them independent, even of the Crown. This was in stark contrast to the Officers of Excise, in whom trust was invested by oath but not by the size of their salary. Paine used some of his best literary devices in this section, showing his understanding of human nature. He also gave insight into the fact that an understanding of reduced circumstances could only be experienced by living in them; if one was not actually in poverty it would be very hard to understand what motivated fraud. Paine claimed that it was indeed not fraud or corruption at all if a human was placed in poverty, but rather a necessary means of keeping alive by any method available. Paine knew that he would be appealing to those who had never been subject to the kind of privation suffered daily by the Officers of Excise.

Paine argued that Excise Officers had the instinct of frailty as well the rest of mankind:

> 'The tenderness of conscience is too often overmatched by the sharpness of want; and principle, like charity, yields with just reluctance enough to excuse itself......No argument can satisfy the feelings of hunger, or abate the edge of appetite. Nothing tends to a greater corruption of manners and principles, than a too great distress of circumstances; and the corruption is of that kind, that it spreads a plaster for itself: like a viper, it carries a cure, though a false one, for its own poison.'

Paine pressed the case that corruption was caused by the circumstances that the Excise Service placed its officers in and not by a character trait of any individual officer. It was a theme throughout this section that the rules surrounding pay and the removal of officers inevitably led to officers being dishonest to survive and that, meanwhile, those in power were unable to comprehend what it was like to be in poverty. Paine was adroit in his use of geography to invoke imagery in the study of human behaviour:

> 'The rich, in ease and affluence, may think I have drawn an unnatural portrait; but could they descend to the cold regions of want, the circle of polar poverty, they would find their opinions changing with the climate. There are habits of thinking peculiar to different conditions, and to find them out is truly to study mankind.'[98]

---

[99] Thomas Paine, *The Case of the Officers of Excise* (Lewes, 1772), p. 12.

The point that the salary had been fixed for a hundred years was next made: *'If the salary was judged competent an hundred years ago, it cannot be so now.'* Paine posed the question, would the government want them to work for nothing? The answer would be no, *'that as they could not live on the salary, they would discretionally live out of the duty.'* Paine mentioned that there were 3,000 Officers of Excise collecting £5,000,000 of duty. On average, each officer collected around £1666 in duty each, totally out of proportion to the salary that they were paid. The arguments mounted. The salary had been fixed at £50 per annum for a hundred years, and had been further reduced by taxation and deductions. There had been rapid inflation of late. The amount of revenue collected was out of all proportion to the salary paid, and there was little chance of earning more by promotion. Other branches of government earned more for doing less; customs men could claim a bounty for contraband seized, but there was no such prize for the Excise Officers:

> *'Poor and in power, are powerful temptations; I call it power, because they* [Officers of Excise] *have it in their power to defraud.....to relieve their wants would be charity, but to secure the revenue by so doing would be prudence. Scarce a week passes at the office but some detections are made of fraudulent and collusive proceedings......The revenue suffers more by the corruption of a few officers in a county, than would make a handsome addition to the salary of the whole number in the same place.'*[99]

Paine urged again for higher pay, this time by charitable prudence. He must have had sight of the minute book or at least have been informed about the weekly frequency of discipline. Paine had knowledge of the collapse of the Cornwall Collection (mentioned earlier, with three Supervisors and the Collector censured) from London and also from John Dewick, the Supervisor who was demoted and moved to Lewes, where Paine was already in post, in July 1768. The argument continued in more descriptive prose:

> *'The bread of deceit is a bread of bitterness; but alas! How few in times of want and hardship are capable of thinking so: objects appear under new colours, and in shapes not naturally their own; hunger sucks in the deception, and necessity reconciles it to conscience.'*[100]

Although not a term used in the 18c, Paine here used psychology to great effect. The mind-bending effect of privation could distort perception. The language Paine used was not technical; he made his point by using ordinary language. We see examples of this throughout *The Case*, including a quote from Shakespeare:

---

[99] Thomas Paine, *The Case of the Officers of Excise* (Lewes, 1772), pp. 13-14.

[100] Thomas Paine, *The Case of the Officers of Excise* (Lewes, 1772), p. 14.

> 'Poverty, like grief, has an incurable deafness, which never hears; the ora-
> tion loses all its edge; and **"To be, or not to be,"** becomes the only ques-
> tion. There is a striking difference between dishonesty arising from want
> of food, and want of principle. The first is worthy of compassion, the
> other of punishment. Nature never produced a Man who would starve in
> a well stored larder, because the provisions were not his own: but he who
> robs it from luxury of appetite deserves a gibbet.'[101]

There is a summing up, an overview, towards the end of this passage that is
damning to the Service, and on the face of it, to those who were in charge.
What is perhaps surprising about the whole of *The Case* is that if it was instructed from the highest level, by the Commissioners, it sometimes appeared
as an attack on the very same administration:

> 'Persons first coming into the Excise form very different notions of it, to
> what they have afterwards. The gay ideas of promotion soon expire. The
> continuance of work, the strictness of the duty, and the poverty of the
> salary, soon beget negligence and indifference: the course continues for a
> while, the revenue suffers, and the officer is discharged: the vacancy is
> soon filled up, new ones arise to produce the same mischief, and share
> the same fate.'[102]

Finally, Paine made another personal observation about the indifference to
being discharged from the service. He moved to teaching after being discharged from the Grantham Collection:

> 'The easy transition of a qualified officer to a Counting-House, or at
> least a School-Master, at any time...naturally supports and backs his in-
> difference about the Excise, so that it takes off all punishment from the
> Order whenever it happens. I have known numbers discharged from the
> Excise, who would have been a credit to their patrons and the employ-
> ment, could they have found it worth their while to have attended to it.
> **No Man enters into the Excise with any higher expectations than a
> competent Maintenance; but to not find even that, can produce
> nothing but Corruption, Collusion, and Neglect.'**[103]

Remarks on the Qualifications of Officers

---

[101] Thomas Paine, *The Case of the Officers of Excise* (Lewes, 1772), pp. 15-16.

[102] Thomas Paine, *The Case of the Officers of Excise* (Lewes, 1772), p. 16.

[103] Thomas Paine, *The Case of the Officers of Excise* (Lewes, 1772), p. 17.

The poor quality of candidates now available to work in the Excise Service was made evident in this section. The pay was now so low all they could recruit were *'the dregs.'* If the pay was lower than a labourer could earn, what could the Service expect? A distinction was made between direct labour, for example cutting a river or making a road, and being placed in a position of trust. In the former, the possibility of fraud was impossible, but in the latter, trust was all: *'A known thief may be trusted to gather stones: but a steward ought to be proof against the temptations of uncounted gold.'* Officers of Excise were expected to be honest, sober, diligent, and skilful. There are many examples in the minute book showing that a want of any of these qualities led to immediate discharge.

Paine claimed that now, due to the insufficiency of salary, anyone of any capacity or reputation would keep out of it. Anyone could earn that daily rate anywhere in any case. A recent example was given where a past Commissioner had openly advertised positions. Only one candidate came forward and he had not made the grade as a tailor's apprentice after seven years. After 12 months training in the Excise he found the real job beyond his capabilities and left.

A distinction was made between the past and the present:

> *'Of Late years there has been such an admission of improper and ill-qualified persons into the Excise, that the office is not only become contemptible, but the revenue insecure. Collectors, whose long service and qualifications have advanced them to that station, are disgraced by the wretchedness of new supernumeraries continually...for what can be more destructive in a revenue office, than CORRUPTION, COLLUSION, NEGLECT, and ILL-QUALIFICATIONS.'*[104]

Also in deference to the present Board:

> *'Of late years the Board of Excise has shewn an extraordinary tenderness in such instances as might otherwise have affected the circumstances of their officers. Their compassion have greatly tended to lessen the distresses of the employment: but as it cannot amount to a total removal of them, the Officers of Excise throughout the kingdom have (as the voice of one Man) prepared petitions to be laid before the honourable House of Commons on the ensuing parliament.'*[105]

In this way, Paine was able to lay open the iniquities of the Excise but at the same time protect the current Board of Commissioners. The blame was laid

---

[104] Thomas Paine, *The Case of the Officers of Excise* (Lewes, 1772), p. 20.

[105] Thomas Paine, *The Case of the Officers of Excise* (Lewes, 1772), pp. 20-21.

on the inability of past administrations to adapt to a changing world. As a final flourish to *The Case,* Paine laid out a bright new future; he identified finally that low pay was at the root of all the problems. In the two final paragraphs Paine pulled it all together:

> *'An augmentation of salary sufficient to enable them to live honestly and competently, would produce more good effect than all the laws of the land can enforce.* **The generality of such frauds as the officers have been detected in, have appeared of a nature as remote from inherent dishonesty, as a temporary illness is from an incurable disease.** *Surrounded with want, children, and despair, what can the husband or the father do.—No laws compel like Nature—No connections bind like blood.*

> *With an addition of salary, the Excise would wear a new aspect, and recover its former constitution. Languor and neglect would give place to care and cheerfulness. Men of reputation and abilities would seek after it, and finding a comfortable maintenance, would stick to it.* **The unworthy and the incapable would be rejected; the power of superiors be re-established; and laws and instructions receive new force. The officers would be secured from the temptations of poverty, and the revenue from the evils of it;** *the cure would be as extensive as the complaint; and new health out root the present CORRUPTIONS.*

> **FINIS.'**[106]

The rules about pay were reinforced by the Lords of the Treasury in this Treasury minute dated 16 October 1724, written in the reign of George I:

> *'The Lords Commissioners of his Majesty's Treasury finding the salarys on your quarterly bill to Michaelmas 1724 to exceed the salarys on the like bill for the summer quarter preceding, their Lordships desire to know the occasion of the Excess, for although the appointing many officers may be within your province yet their Lordships are of Opinion* **the assigning or increasing salaries ought not to be done but upon a proper Representation to their Lordships in that behalf** *and a warrant thereupon to establish and allow the same.'*[107]

---

[106] Thomas Paine, *The Case of the Officers of Excise* (Lewes, 1772), p. 21.

[107] George Hindmarch, *Thomas Paine: The Case of the King of England and his Officers of Excise* (published privately, 1998), p. 17.

The Officers of Excise in fact had been paid the same salaries since 1683. There is no known discussion recorded about the pay of Excise Officers before the ruling above, nor after in the Excise Commissioners' correspondence with the Treasury until 1773. Not until *The Case of The Officers of Excise* was the matter of pay addressed.

The situation was clearly very frustrating to the Commissioners of Excise. They could not run an efficient service under these circumstances; there was too much energy expended in dispensing with discipline. The Service was failing due to low pay, which led to all the problems of corruption and recruitment. *The Case* exposed the underbelly of a failing nation, as can be seen by Lord North's statement to Parliament that the Treasury was besieged by petitions for higher pay from other government departments. There were petitions from many trades as well, including the Silk Weavers, a notable case that was well-reported in the press.

The Case crowned a sustained effort due to the time it took to collect all the signatures. The argument was articulated fully and in depth by the chosen writer. It blew the whistle on the poor practice of the largest government department. It was a failure of government writ large, orchestrated by the department's top employees, the Commissioners of Excise; they must have sanctioned Paine's content. That content exposed a failing department. It was a very brave move. This makes sense of their cautious step-by-step approach; the earlier petitions were sent directly to the Lords of the Treasury, the final petition being much more organised and sent via the Excise Office. *The Case* was not mentioned in the covering letter from the Excise Commissioners, perhaps to maintain a distance from it, but Paine mentioned the petition from the committee of eight in *The Case*.

Colin Brent concluded that Paine's vision in *The Case* was embodied later in the Home and Imperial Civil Service fashioned by the Victorians.[108] Most of Paine's recommendations were adopted over time; the expense of horse keeping was reimbursed, the practice of removing officers to all over the country was stopped and eventually pay was brought into line with the national economy.[109]

A world first: the campaign and *The Case* represented the first national union of workers anywhere in the world.

---

[108] Colin Brent, 'Thirty Something: Thomas Paine at Bull House in Lewes, 1768-74 - Six Formative Years', *Sussex Archaeological Society Collections,* vol. 147 (2009), pp. 153-67.

[109] Graham Smith, *Something to Declare: 1000 years of Customs and Excise* (London, 1980), p. 107.

The Original Case of the Officers of Excise

T H E

C A S E

OF THE

OFFICERS

O F

E X C I S E;

With REMARKS on the

QUALIFICATIONS

O F

OFFICERS;

AND ON THE

Numerous EVILS arifing to the

REVENUE,

From the INSUFFICIENCY of the

PRESENT SALARY.

Humbly addreffed to the

HON. and RIGHT HON. the MEMBERS

O F

BOTH HOUSES of PARLIAMENT.

[iii]

THE

INTRODUCTION.

A S a Defign among the Excife Officers throughout the Kingdom is on Foot, for an humble
Application to Parliament next Seffion, to have the
State of their Salaries taken into Confideration ; it
has been judged not only expedient, but highly neceffary to prefent a State of their Cafe, previous to
the Prefentation of their Petition.

There are fome Cafes fo fingularly reafonable,
that the more they are confidered, the more Weight
they obtain. It is a ftrong Evidence both of Simplicity, and honeft Confidence, when Petitioners in any Cafe, ground their Hopes of Relief,
on having their Cafe fully and perfectly known and
underftood.

Simple as this Subject may appear at firft, it is
a Matter, in my humble Opinion, not unworthy
a Parliamentary Attention. 'Tis a Subject inter-
woven with a Variety of Reafons from different
Caufes. New Matter will arife on every Thought.
*If the Poverty of the Officers of Excife ; if the Temptations
arifing from their Poverty ; if the Qualifications of Perfons to be admitted into the Employment ; if the Security of*

A 2   *the*

[iv]

the Revenue itself, are Matters of any Weight, then I am conscious that my voluntary Services in this Business, will produce some good Effect or other, either to the better Security of the Revenue, the Relief of the Officers, or both.

THE

[5]

T H E

S T A T E,

Of the S A L A R Y

Of the *Officers* of E X C I S E.

WHEN a Year's Salary is mentioned in the Grofs, it acquires a Degree of Confequence from its *Sound,* which it would not have if feparated into daily Payments, and if the Charges attend-ing the receiving, and other unavoidable Expences were confidered with it. Fifty Pounds a Year, and One Shil-ling and Ninepence Farthing a Day, carry as different Degrees of Significancy with them, as My Lord's Steward, and the Steward's Labourer; and yet an Out-Ride Offi-cer in the Excife, under the Name of Fifty Pounds a Year receives for himfelf no more than One Shilling and Ninepence Farthing a Day.

After Tax, Charity, and fitting Expences are deducted, there remains very little more than Forty-fix Pounds; and the Expences of Horfe-keeping in many Places cannot be brought under Fourteen Pounds a Year, be-fides the Purchafe at firft, and the Hazard of Life, which reduces it to Thirty-two Pounds *per Annum,* or One Shilling and Ninepence Farthing *per* Day.

B   I have

[6]

I have fpoken more particularly of the Out-Rides, as they are by far the moft numerous, being in Proportion to the Foot-Walks as Eight is to Five throughout the Kingdom. Yet in the latter the fame Misfortunes exift; the Channel of them only is altered. The exceffive dearnefs of Houfe-rent, the great Burthen of Rates and Taxes, and the exceffive Price of all the Neceffaries of Life, in Cities and large Trading Towns, nearly counter-balance the Expences of Horfe-keeping. Every Office has its Stages of Promotion, but the pecuniary Advantages arifing from a Foot-Walk are fo inconfiderable, and the Lofs of difpofing of Effects, or the Charges of removing them to any confiderable Diftance fo great, that many Out-ride Officers with a Family remain as they are, from an Inability to bear the Lofs, or fupport the Expence.

The Officers refident in the Cities of *London* and *Weftminfter*, are exempt from the particular Difadvantages of Removals. This feems to be the only Circumftance which they enjoy fuperior to their Country Brethren. In every other refpect they lay under the fame Hardfhips, and fuffer the fame Diftreffes.

There are no Perquifites or Advantages in the leaft, annexed to the Employment. A few Officers who are ftationed along the Coaft, may fometimes have the good Fortune to fall in with a Seizure of contraband Goods, and yet, that frequently at the Hazard of their Lives: But the inland Officers can have no fuch Opportunities. Befides, the furveying Duty in the Excife is fo continual, that without Remiffnefs from the real Bufinefs itfelf, there is no Time to feek after them. With the Officers of the Cuftoms it is quite otherwife, their whole Time and Care is appropriated to that Service, and their Profits are in proportion to their Vigilance.

If the Increafe of Money in the Kingdom is one Caufe of the high Price of Provifions, the Cafe of the Excife-Officers is peculiarly pitiable. No Increafe comes to them ——They are fhut out from the general Bleffing——

They

[7]

They behold it like a Map of *Peru*———The Anſwer of *Abraham* to *Dives* is ſomewhat applicable to them, " *There is a great Gulf fix'd.*"

To the Wealthy and Humane, it is a Matter worthy of Concern, that their Affluence ſhould become the Misfortune of others. Were the Money in the Kingdom to be increaſed double, the Salary would in Value be reduced one half. Every Step upwards, is a Step downwards with them. Not to be Partakers of the Increaſe would be a little hard, but to be Sufferers by it is exceedingly ſo. The Mechanic and the Labourer may in a great Meaſure ward off the Diſtreſs, by raiſing the Price of their Manufactures or their Work, but the Situation of the Officers, admit of no ſuch Relief.

Another Conſideration in their Behalf (and which is peculiar to the Exciſe) is, that as the Law of their Office removes them far from all their natural Friends and Relations, it conſequently prevents thoſe occaſional Aſſiſtances from them, which are ſerviceably felt in a Family, and which even the pooreſt, among the Poor enjoys. Moſt poor Mechanics, or even common Labourers, have ſome Relations or Friends, who, either out of Benevolence, or Pride, keep their Children from Nakedneſs, ſupply them occaſionally with perhaps half a Hog, a Load of Wood, a Chaldron of Coals, or ſomething or other which abates the Severity of their Diſtreſs, and yet thoſe Men thus relieved will frequently earn, more than the daily Pay of an Exciſe Officer.

Perhaps an Officer will appear more reputable with the ſame Pay than a Mechanic or Labourer. The difference ariſes from Sentiment, not Circumſtances. A ſomething like reputable Pride makes all the Diſtinction, and the thinking Part of Mankind well knows, that none ſuffer ſo much as they who endeavour to conceal their Neceſſities.

The frequent Removals which unavoidably happen in the Exciſe, are attended with ſuch an Expence, eſpecially

B 2   where

[8]

where there is a Family, as few Officers are able to support. About two Years ago an Officer with a Family, under Orders for removing, and rather embarraffed Circumftances, made his Application to me, and from a Conviction of his Diftrefs, I advanced a fmall Sum to enable him to proceed. He ingenuoufly declared, that without the Affiftance of fome Friend, he fhould be driven to do Injuftice to his Creditors, and compelled to defert the Duty of his Office. He has fince honeftly paid me, and does as well as the Narrownefs of fuch Circumftances can admit of.

There is one general allowed Truth, which will always operate in their Favour, which is, that no Set of Men under his Majefty, earn their Salary with any Comparifon of Labour and Fatigue with that of the Officers of Excife. The Station may rather be called a Seat of conftant Work, than either a Place, or an Employment. Even in the different Departments of the general Revenue they are unequalled in the Burthen of Bufinefs; a Riding-Officer's Place in the Cuftoms, whofe Salary is 60 l. a Year, is *Eafe* to theirs; and the Work in the Window-Light Duty, compared with the Excife, is *Lightnefs itfelf*, yet their Salary is fubject to no Tax, they receive Forty-nine Pounds Twelve Shillings and Sixpence, without Deduction.

The Inconveniencies which affect an Excife Officer are almoft endlefs; even the Land Tax Affeffment upon their Salaries, which though the Government pays, falls often with Hardfhip upon them. The Place of their Refidence, on account of the Land Tax, has in many Inftances created frequent Contentions between Parifhes, in which the Officer, though the innocent and unconcerned Caufe of the Quarrel, has been the greater Sufferer.

To point out particularly the Impoffibility of an Excife Officer fupporting himfelf and Family, with any proper Degree of Credit and Reputation, on fo fcanty a Pittance, is altogether unneceffary. The Times, the Voice of general

[9]

neral Want, is Proof itfelf. Where Facts are fufficient, Arguments are ufelefs; and the Hints which I have produced are fuch as affect the Officers of Excife *differently* to any other Set of Men. A fingle Man may barely live; but as it is not the Defign of the Legiflature, or the Honourable Board of Excife, to impofe a State of Celibacy on them, the Condition of much the greater Part is truly wretched and pitiable.

Perhaps it may be faid, Why do the Excife Officers complain; they are not preffed into the Service, and may relinquifh it when they pleafe; if they can mend themfelves, why don't they? Alas! what a Mockery of Pity would it be; to give fuch an Anfwer to an honeft, faithful old Officer in the Excife, who had fpent the Prime of his Life in the Service, and was become unfit for any Thing elfe. The Time limited for an Admiffion into an Excife Employment, is between twenty-one and thirty Years of Age—the very Flower of Life. Every other Hope and Confideration is then given up, and the Chance of eftablifhing themfelves in any other Bufinefs, becomes in a few Years not only loft to them, but they become loft to it.

    " There is a Tide in the Affairs of Men, which if
    " embraced, leads on to Fortune——*That neglected*, all
    " beyond is Mifery or Want."

When we confider how few in the Excife arrive at any comfortable Eminence, and the Date of Life when fuch Promotions only can happen, the great Hazard there is of ill, rather than good Fortune in the Attempt, and that all the Years antecedent to that is a State of mere Exiftence, wherein they are fhut out from the common Chance of Succefs in any other Way; a Reply like that can be only a Derifion of their Wants. 'Tis almoft impoffible after any long Continuance in the Excife, that they *can* live any other Way. Such as are of Trades, would have their Trade to learn over again; and People would have but little Opinion of their Abilities in any Calling, who had been

[10]

been ten, fifteen, or twenty Years abfent from it. Every Year's Experience gained in the Excife, is a Year's Experience loft in Trade; and by the Time they become wife Officers, they become foolifh Workmen.

Were the Reafons for augmenting the Salary grounded only on the Charitablenefs of fo doing, they would have great Weight with the Compaffionate. But there are Auxiliaries of fuch a powerful Caft, that in the Opinion of Policy, they obtain the Rank of Originals. The firft is truly the Cafe of the Officers, but this is rather the Cafe of the Revenue.

The Diftreffes in the Excife are fo generally known, that Numbers of Gentlemen, and other Inhabitants in Places where Officers are refident, have generoufly and humanely recommended their Cafe to the Members of the Honourable Houfe of Commons: And Numbers of Traders of Opulence and Reputation, well knowing that the Poverty of an Officer may fubject him to the fraudulent Defigns of fome felfifh Perfons under his Survey, to the great Injury of the fair Trader, and Trade in general, have, from Principles both of Generofity and Juftice, joined in the fame Recommendation.

THOUGHTS

[11]

THOUGHTS

On the Corruption of Principles, and on the numerous Evils

Arising to the Revenue from the too great Poverty of the *Officers* of *Excise*.

IT has always been the Wisdom of Government to con-sider the Situation and Circumstances of Persons in Trust. Why are large Salaries given in many Instances, but to proportion it to the Trust, to set Men above Temptation, and to make it even literally worth their while to be honest. The Salaries of the Judges have been augmented, and their Places made independent even on the Crown itself, for the above wise Purposes.

Certainly there can be nothing unreasonable in supposing there is such an Instinct as Frailty among the Officers of Excise, in common with the rest of Mankind; and that the most effectual Method to keep Men honest, is to enable them to live so. The Tenderness of Conscience is too often overmatched by the Sharpness of Want; and Principle, like Chastity, yields with just Reluctance

[12]

Reluctance enough to excuse itself. There is a powerful Rhetorick in Neceſſity, which exceeds even a *Dunning*, or a *Wedderburne*. No Argument can ſatisfy the Feelings of Hunger, or abate the Edge of Appetite. Nothing tends to a greater Corruption of Manners and Principles, than a too great Diſtreſs of Circumſtances; and the Corruption is of that Kind, that it ſpreads a Plaiſter for itſelf: Like a Viper, it carries a Cure, though a falſe one, for its own Poiſon. *Agur*, without any Alternative, has made Diſhoneſty the immediate Conſequence of Poverty, " Left I be poor and ſteal." A very little Degree of that dangerous Kind of Philoſophy, which is the almoſt certain Effect of involuntary Poverty, will teach Men to believe, that to ſtarve is more criminal than to ſteal, by as much as every Species of Self-Murder exceeds every other Crime; that true Honeſty is ſentimental, and the Practice of it dependent upon Circumſtances. If the Gay find it difficult to reſiſt the Allurements of Pleaſure; the Great the Temptations of Ambition; or the Miſer the Acquiſition of Wealth; how much ſtronger are the Provocations of Want and Poverty. The Excitements to Pleaſure, Grandeur, or Riches, are mere " Shadows of a " Shade," compared to the irreſiſtable Neceſſities of Nature. Not to be led into Temptation, is the Prayer of Divinity itſelf; and to guard againſt, or rather to prevent ſuch inſnaring Situations, is one of the greateſt Heights of Human Prudence: In private Life it is partly religious; and in a Revenue Senſe, it is truly political.

The Rich, in Eaſe and Affluence, may think I have drawn an unnatural Portrait; but could they deſcend to the cold Regions of Want, the Circle of Polar Poverty, they would find their Opinions changing with the Climate. There are Habits of Thinking peculiar to different Conditions, and to find them out is truly to ſtudy Mankind.

That the Situation of an Exciſe Officer is of this dangerous Kind, muſt be allowed by every one who will conſider

fider the Truft unavoidably repofed In him, and compare
the Narrownefs of his Circumftances with the Hardfhip
of the Times. If the Salary was judged competent an
Hundred Years ago, it cannot be fo now. Should it be
advanced, that if the prefent Set of Officers are diffatisfied
with the Salary, that enow may be procured not only
for the prefent Salary, but for lefs; the Anfwer is extremely eafy. The Queftion needs only be put; it de-
ftroys itfelf. Were Two or Three Thoufand Men to
offer to execute the Office without any Salary, would the
Government accept them? No. Were the fame Number
to offer the fame Service for a Salary lefs than can poffibly
fupport them, would the Government accept them? Certainly No; for while Nature, in fpite of Law or Religion, makes it a ruling Principle not to ftarve, the Event
would be this; that as they could not live on the Salary,
they would difcretionarily live out of the Duty. Quære,
whether Poverty has not too great an Influence now?
Were the Employment a Place of direct Labour, and not
of Truft, then Frugality in the Salary would be found
Policy: But when it is confidered that the greateft fingle
Branch of the Revenue, a Duty amounting to near Five
Millions Sterling, is annually charged by a Set of Men,
moft of whom are wanting even the common Neceffaries
of Life, the Thought muft to every Friend to Honefty,
to every Perfon concerned in the Management of the Public Money, be ftrong and ftriking. Poor and in Power,
are powerful Temptations; I call it Power, becaufe they
have it in their Power to defraud. The Truft unavoidably repofed in an Excife Officer is fo great, that it would
be an Act of Wifdom, and perhaps of Intereft, to fecure
him from the Temptations of downright Poverty. To
relieve their Wants would be Charity, but to fecure the
Revenue by fo doing would be Prudence. Scarce a Week
paffes at the Office but fome Detections are made of fraudulent and collufive Proceedings. The Poverty of the Officers

[14]

cers is the faireſt Bait for a deſigning Trader that can poſſibly be; ſuch introduce themſelves to the Officer under the common Plea of the Inſufficiency of the Salary. Every conſiderate Mind muſt allow, that Poverty and Opportunity corrupt many an honeſt Man. I am not at all ſurpriſed that ſo many opulent and reputable Traders have recommended the Caſe of the Officers to the good Favour of their Repreſentatives. They are ſenſible of the pinching Circumſtances of the Officers, and of the Injury to Trade in general from the Advantages which are taken of them. The Welfare of the fair Trader and the Security of the Revenue are ſo inſeparably one, that their Intereſts or Injuries are alike. It is the Opinion of ſuch whoſe Situation give them a perfect Knowledge in the Matter, that the Revenue ſuffers more by the Corruption of a few Officers in a County, than would make a handſome Addition to the Salary of the whole Number in the ſame Place.

I very lately knew an Inſtance where it is evident, on Compariſon of the Duty charged ſince, that the Revenue ſuffered by one Trader (and he not a very conſiderable one) upwards of One Hundred and Sixty Pounds *per Annum* for ſeveral Years; and yet the Benefit to the Officer was a mere Trifle, in Conſideration of the Trader's. Without Doubt the Officer would have thought himſelf much happier to have received the ſame Addition another Way. The Bread of Deceit is a Bread of Bitterneſs; but alas! how few in Times of Want and Hardſhip are capable of thinking ſo: Objects appear under new Colours, and in Shapes not naturally their own; Hunger ſucks in the Deception, and Neceſſity reconciles it to Conſcience.

The Commiſſioners of Exciſe ſtrongly enjoin that no Officer accept any Treat, Gratuity, or, in ſhort, lay himſelf under any kind of Obligation to the Traders under their Survey: The Wiſdom of ſuch an Injunction is evident,

evident; but the Practice of it, to a Perſon ſurrounded with Children and Poverty, is ſcarcely poſſible; and ſuch Obligations, wherever they exiſt, muſt operate, directly, or indirectly, to the Injury of the Revenue. Favours will naturally beget their Likeneſſes, eſpecially where the Return is not at our own Expence.

I have heard it remarked by a Gentleman whoſe Knowledge in Exciſe Buſineſs is indiſputable, that there are Numbers of Officers who are even afraid to look into an unentered Room, leſt they ſhould give Offence. Poverty and Obligation tye up the Hands of Office, and give a prejudicial Bias to the Mind.

There is another kind of Evil, which, though it may never amount to what may be deemed Criminality in Law, yet it may amount to what is much worſe in Effect, and that is, *a conſtant and perpetual Leakage in the Revenue*: A Sort of Gratitude in the Dark, a diſtant Requital for ſuch Civilities as only the loweſt Poverty would accept, and which are a Thouſand *per Cent.* above the Value of the Civility received. Yet here is no immediate Colluſion; the Trader and Officer are both ſafe, the Deſign, if diſcovered, paſſes for Error.

Theſe, with numberleſs other Evils, have all their Origin in the Poverty of the Officers. Poverty, in Defiance of Principle, begets a Degree of Meanneſs that will ſtoop to almoſt any Thing. A thouſand Refinements of Argument may be brought to prove, that the Practice of Honeſty will be ſtill the ſame, in the moſt trying and neceſſitous Circumſtances. He who never was an hunger'd may argue finely on the Subjection of his Appetite; and he who never was diſtreſſed, may harangue as beautifully on the Power of Principle. But Poverty, like Grief, has an incurable Deafneſs, which *never hears*; the Oration loſes all its Edge; and " *To be, or not to be,* becomes the only Queſtion.

C 2

There

[16]

There is a ſtriking Difference between Diſhoneſty ariſing from Want of Food, and Want of Principle. The firſt is worthy of Compaſſion, the other of Puniſhment. Nature never produced a Man who would ſtarve in a well ſtored Larder, becauſe the Proviſions were not his own: But he who robs it from Luxury of Appetite deſerves a Gibbet.

There is another Evil which the Poverty of the Salary produces, and which nothing but an Augmentation of it can remove; and that is, Negligence and Indifference. Theſe may not appear of ſuch dark Complexion as Fraud, and Colluſion, but their Injuries to the Revenue are the ſame. It is impoſſible that any Office or Buſineſs can be regarded as it ought, where this ruinous Diſpoſition ex-iſts. It requires no ſort of Argument to prove that the Value ſet upon any Place or Employment will be in Pro-portion to the Value of it; and that Diligence or Neg-ligence will ariſe from the ſame Cauſe. The continual Number of Relinquiſhments and Diſcharges always hap-pening in the Exciſe, are evident Proofs of it.

Perſons firſt coming into the Exciſe form very different Notions of it, to what they have afterwards. The gay Ideas of Promotion ſoon expire. The Continuance of Work, the Strictneſs of the Duty, and the Poverty of the Salary, ſoon beget Negligence and Indifference: The Courſe continues for a while, the Revenue ſuffers, and the Officer is diſcharged: The Vacancy is ſoon filled up, new ones ariſe to produce the ſame Miſchief, and ſhare the ſame Fate.

What adds ſtill more to the Weight of this Grievance is, that this deſtructive Diſpoſition reigns moſt among ſuch as are otherwiſe the moſt proper and qualified for the Employment; ſuch as are neither fit for the Exciſe, or any Thing elſe, are glad to hold in by any Means: But the Revenue lies at as much Hazard from their Want of Judgment, as from the other's Want of Diligence.

In

In private Life no Man would truſt the Execution of
any important Concern, to a Servant who was careleſs
whether he did it or not, and the ſame Rule muſt hold
good in a Revenue Senſe. The Commiſſioners may con-
tinue diſcharging every Day, and the Example will have
no Weight while the Salary is an Object ſo inconſiderable,
and this Diſpoſition has ſuch a general Exiſtence. Should
it be advanced, that if Men will be careleſs of ſuch
Bread as is in their Poſſeſſion, they will ſtill be the ſame
were it better; I anſwer, that as the Diſpoſition I am
ſpeaking of, is not the Effect of natural Idleneſs, but
of Diſſatisfaction in point of Profit, they would *not* con-
tinue the ſame. A good Servant will be careful of a good
Place, though very indifferent about a bad one. Beſides,
this Spirit of Indifference, ſhould it procure a Diſcharge,
is no ways affecting to their Circumſtances. The eaſy
Tranſition of a qualified Officer to a 'Compting-Houſe,
or at leaſt a School-Maſter, at any Time, as it naturally
ſupports and backs his Indifference about the Exciſe, ſo
it takes off all Puniſhment from the Order whenever it
happens.

I have known Numbers diſcharged from the Exciſe,
who would have been a Credit to their Patrons and the
Employment, could they have found it worth their while
to have attended to it. No Man enters into the Exciſe
with any higher Expectations than a competent Maintenance; but not to find even that, can produce nothing
but *Corruption*, *Colluſion*, and *Neglect*.

REMARKS

[18]

REMARKS

ON THE

QUALIFICATIONS of OFFICERS.

IN Employments where direct Labour only is wanting, and Truft quite out of the Queftion, the Service is merely animal or mechanical.——In cutting a River, or forming a Road, as there is no Poffibility of Fraud, the Merit of Honefty is but of little Weight. Health, Strength, and Hardinefs, are the Labourers Virtues. But where Property depends on the Truft, and lies at the Difcretion of the Servant, the Judgment of the Mafter takes a different Channel, both in the Choice and the Wages. The Honeft and the Diffolute have here no Comparifon of Merit. A known Thief may be trufted to gather Stones : But a Steward ought to be Proof againft the Temptations of uncounted Gold.

The Excife is fo far from being of the Nature of the firft, that it is all, and more, than can commonly be put together in the laft: 'Tis a Place of *Poverty, of Truft, of Opportunity, and Temptation.* A Compound of Difcords, where the more they harmonize, the more they offend. Ruin and Reconcilement are produced at once.

To be properly qualified for the Employment, it is not only neceffary that the Perfon fhould be honeft, but that he

be

be fober, diligent, and fkilful: Sober, that he may be always capable of Bufinefs; diligent, that he may be always in his Bufinefs; and fkilful, that he may be able to prevent or detect Frauds againft the Revenue. The Want of any of thefe Qualifications is a Capital Offence in the Excife. A Complaint of Drunkennefs, Negligence, or Ignorance, is certain Death by the Laws of the Board. It cannot then be all Sorts of Perfons who are proper for the Office. The very Notion of procuring a fufficient Number for even lefs than the prefent Salary, is fo deftitute of every Degree of found Reafon, that it needs no Reply. The Employment, from the Infufficiency of the Salary, is *already* become fo inconfiderable in the general Opinion, that Perfons of any Capacity or Reputation will keep out of it; for where is the Mechanic, or even the Labourer, who cannot earn at leaft 1 s. 9 d. Farthing *per* Day? It certainly cannot be proper to take the Dregs of every Calling, and to make the Excife the common Receptacle for the Indigent, the Ignorant, and the Calamitous.

A truly worthy Commiffioner lately dead, made a public Offer a few Years ago, of putting any of his Neighbours Sons into the Excife; but though the Offer amounted almoft to an Invitation, one only, whom feven Years Apprenticefhip could not make a Taylor, accepted it; who, after a Twelvemonth's Inftruction, was ordered off, but in a few Days finding the Employment beyond his Abilities, he prudently deferted it, and returned Home, where he now remains in the Character of an Hufbandman.

There are very few Inftances of Rejection even of Perfons who can fcarce write their own Names legible; for as there is neither Law to compel, nor Encouragement to incite, no other can be had than fuch as offer, and none will offer who can fee any other Profpect of Living. Every one knows that the Excife is a Place of Labour,

not

[20]

not of Eafe; of Hazard, not of Certainty; and that downright Poverty finifhes the Character.

It muft ftrike every confiderate Mind to hear a Man, with a large Family faithful enough to declare, that he cannot fupport himfelf on the Salary with that honeft Independance he could wifh. There is a great Degree of affecting Honefty in an ingenuous Confeffion. Eloquence may ftrike the Ear, but the Language of Poverty ftrikes the Heart; the firft may charm like Mufic, but the fecond alarms like a Knell.

Of late Years there has been fuch an Admiffion of improper and ill qualified Perfons into the Excife, that the Office is not only become contemptible, but the Revenue infecure. Collectors, whofe long Services and Qualifications have advanced them to that Station, are difgraced by the Wretchednefs of new Supers continually. Certainly fome Regard ought to be had to Decency, as well as Merit.

Thefe are fome of the capital Evils which arife from the wretched Poverty of the Salary. Evils they certainly are; for what can be more deftructive in a Revenue Office, than CORRUPTION, COLLUSION, NEGLECT, and ILL QUALIFICATIONS.

Should it be queftioned whether an Augmentation of Salary would remove them, I anfwer, there is fcarce a Doubt to be made of it. Human Wifdom may poffibly be deceived in its wifeft Defigns; but here, every Thought and Circumftance eftablifh the Hope. They are Evils of fuch a ruinous Tendency, that they muft, by fome Means or other, be removed. Rigour and Severity have been tried in vain; for Punifhment lofes all its Force where Men expect and difregard it.

Of late Years the Board of Excife has fhewn an extraordinary Tendernefs in fuch Inftances as might otherwife have affected the Circumftances of their Officers. Their Compaffion have greatly tended to leffen the Diftreffes of

[21]

of the Employment: But as it cannot amount to a total Re-moval of them, the Officers of Excife throughout the Kingdom have (as the Voice of one Man) prepared Peti-tions to be laid before the Hon. Houfe of Commons on the enfuing Parliament.

An Augmentation of Salary fufficient to enable them to live honeftly and competently, would produce more good Effect than all the Laws of the Land can enforce. The Generality of fuch Frauds as the Officers have been detected in, have appeared of a Nature as remote from in-herent Difhonefty, as a temporary Illnefs is from an in-curable Difeafe. Surrounded with *Want*, *Children*, and *Defpair*, what can the *Hufband* or the *Father* do.——No Laws compel like Nature——No Connections bind like Blood.

With an Addition of Salary, the Excife would wear a new Afpect, and recover its former Conftitution. Lan-guor and Neglect would give Place to Care and Chearful-nefs. Men of Reputation and Abilities would feek after it, and finding a comfortable Maintenance, would ftick to it. The unworthy and the incapable would be re-jected; the Power of Superiors be re-eftablifhed; and Laws and Inftructions receive new Force. The Officers would be fecured from the Temptations of Poverty, and the Revenue from the Evils of it; the Cure would be as extenfive as the Complaint; and new Health out-root the prefent CORRUPTIONS.

F I N I S.

The Oaths

The Oath of Allegiance:

> *I, Thomas Paine, do sincerely promise and swear, that I will be faithful
> and bear true Allegiance to his Majesty King George;*
> *So help me God.*

The Oath of Supremacy:

> *I, Thomas Paine, do sincerely promise and swear, That I do, from my
> Heart, Abhor, Detest, and abjure, as impious and heretical, that
> Damnable Doctrine and Position, that Princes excommunicated or de-
> prived by the Pope, or any Authority of the See of Rome, may be deposed
> or murdered by their Subjects, or any other whatsoever. And I do declare,
> that no foreign Prince, Person, Prelate, State or Potentate hath, or ought
> to have, any Jurisdiction, Power, Superiority. Preeminence or Authority,
> Ecclesiastical or Spiritual, within this Realm:*
> *So help me God.*[110]

A third oath was then taken for the faithful execution of duty, and that no
fees or reward would be accepted for services otherwise than from the
Crown. Although the young officer could now commence his duties there
were yet more legal formalities. More oaths were required. The officer swore
the oaths of Test and Abjuration at the next Quarter Sessions of the local
court. This after a qualifying ceremony that had to be enacted in the form of a
sacrament on a Sunday in the presence of two witnesses who also had to appear at the Oaths taken in the Court. The minister and church wardens produced and signed a certificate in front of these witnesses to prove that the
candidate had received the sacrament which the witnesses then produced in
court.

---

[110] Charles Leadbetter, *The Royal Gauger; Or, Gauging Made Perfectly Easy, as it is Actually
Practised by the Officers of His Majesty's Revenue of Excise. In Two Parts.* (London, 1750), p.
216.

The Test Oath:

> 'I, Thomas Paine, do declare, that I do believe there is not any Transub-
> stantiation in the Sacrament of the Lord's Supper, or in the Elements of
> Bread and Wine, at or after the Consecration thereof, by any Person or
> Persons whatsoever.'

The Oath of Abjuration:

> 'I, Thomas Paine, do truly and sincerely acknowledge, profess, testify and
> declare in my Conscience before God and the World, that our Sovereign
> Lord King George is lawful and rightful King of this Realm, and all of his
> Majesty's Dominions thereunto belonging, And I do solemnly and sin-
> cerely declare, That I do believe in my Conscience, that the person pre-
> tended to be Prince of Wales, during the life of the **late King James**, and
> since his Decease pretending to be and taking himself the Style and Title
> of King of England, by the Names of James the Third, or of Scotland by
> the Name of James the Eighth, or the Style and Title of Great Britain,
> hath not any Right or Title whatsoever to the Crown of this Realm.........I
> will do my utmost to disclose .....all Treasons and Traitorous conspiracies
> which I shall know to be against him....'

> 'And I do faithfully promise to the utmost of my power to support, main-
> tain and defend the succession of the Crown **against him the said
> James,** and all other persons whatsoever; which succession (by an **Act**
> entitled, **An Act for the further Limitation of the Crown, and better
> securing the Rights and Liberties of the Subject**) is and stands limit-
> ed to the Princess Sophia, late Electress and Dutchess Dowager of
> Hanover, and the Heirs of her Body, being Protestants. And all of these
> things I do plainly and sincerely acknowledge and swear, according to
> these express Words by me spoken, and according to the same Words,
> **without Equivocation, mental Evasion, or secret Reservation what-
> soever.** And I do make this Recognition, Acknowledgement, Abjuration,
> Renunciation and Promise heartily, willingly and truly, upon the true
> **Faith of a Christian.**'

'William Lee and Lewes printing in the 18th Century,' by Peter Chasseaud. An excerpt from 'The History of Printing in Lewes'

1695, the year that the 1662 Newspaper Licensing Act was permitted to lapse, led to an explosion of printing: by 1709 London had eighteen regular newspapers, and provincial printing spread rapidly. By 1750 over fifty towns had newspapers. The south-east saw the birth of the *Kentish Post or Canterbury News-Letter* in 1717, the *Reading Mercury or Weekly Entertainer* in 1723, the *Essex Mercury and Weekly Journal* in Colchester in 1733, the *Sussex Weekly Advertiser* in Lewes in 1746, and the *Kentish Gazette* in 1768. However, the 1712 Stamp Act, intended to control political pamphlets, had a profound effect on the development of newspapers, leading to over seventy titles disappearing in that year.

Despite being a county town with its own Borough corporation, assizes and quarter sessions, Lewes printing seems to have got off to a slow start, and the first printer in the town was almost certainly Edward Verrall, a bookseller, printer, publisher and stationer from 1731 to 1767, who set up a jobbing printing business and, in 1731 (the earliest recorded printing date for Lewes), was commissioned by the Borough to print public notices about a smallpox outbreak.

In 1745 William Lee (1713-86) of Chichester in west Sussex, who had already been printing in that city and published a newspaper there, set up a press near the top, and on the east side, of Keere Street, Lewes where, in 1746, he began to print the *Sussex Weekly Advertiser; or, Lewes Journal*. Verrall and Lee were briefly in a printing collaboration or partnership in the 1740s. By 1769, and probably earlier, apart from his wooden common press (or presses) for letterpress work, Lee also had a rolling press for printing copper-plate engravings (noted in his imprint to the *Sussex Weekly Advertiser* in January 1769).

All letterpress printing until the end of the 18c was carried out on the wooden common press (with steel screw and bar for pulling, and several other metal parts), the lineal development of Gutenberg's and Caxton's presses of the 15th century. The common press was normally operated by two pressmen who exchanged positions hourly, one 'beating' (inking the forme) with his leather-covered inking balls, and the other 'pulling'. The forme consisted of the set type (e.g. the double page spread of a newspaper, assembled by a compositor on his stone and locked up in an iron frame called a chase. This forme was, in turn, placed onto the bed of the press (a large, flat, rectangular stone housed in a wooden 'coffin', which was wound (using the rounce) on a carriage which slid under the platen.

A pressman or the fly hand took a sheet of dampened paper from a pile and impaled it on two metal points at the middle of each side of the tympan frame, which was hinged at the end of the coffin so that it could be brought down onto the forme. The tympan itself was covered with vellum. To ensure that the paper to be printed was protected from any ink around the edge of the forme, another thin metal frame (the frisket) covered with paper, in which were cut windows to expose the type areas, was hinged to the tympan. Once the paper was impaled, the frisket was swung down onto the tympan, helping to hold the paper in place, and the whole tympan/frisket assembly swung down onto the inked forme, which was then wound under the platen.

The act of pulling the arm turned a screw which exerted downward pressure, via a piston, on the platen, a suspended wooden block, metal-faced, which pressed the dampened paper onto the inked forme. The platen was only large enough to print one page of a spread, so the forme was wound on to bring the second, or facing, page under the platen, and the bar pulled once more; the common press was therefore known as a two-pull press (Gutenberg's was a single-pull, and could only print one page at a time). An apprentice or 'fly-hand' often assisted to handle the paper on and off the press, and hang it up to dry. Two pressmen, beating and pulling, could easily produce 200 sheets an hour (printed on one side of the paper). Once dry, these were then printed, using another forme, on the reverse.

The compositor set the type while standing at his random or frame, the upper (capitals) and lower cases of type in front of him at chest level. Long apprenticeship and habituation meant that he knew thoroughly the 'lay of the case'; each typecase was divided into small wooden boxes containing the different letters, or 'sorts', figures, punctuations marks, spaces, etc., and the compositor would pick out his types and assemble them in his composing stick (set to the right 'measure' or column width), held in this left hand, at amazing speed. Lines of assembled type were transferred to a galley, in which they could be inked and proofread (hence 'galley proofs'). The compositor made corrections in the galley, and last-minute corrections could be made in the forme, after the type had been locked-up in the chase. Once the printing job was completed, the forme was scrubbed with lye (caustic) to remove the ink, dried, and then unlocked so that the type could be distributed back into its cases.

Lee bought his types from that great London typefounder, William Caslon, who produced his own classic version of the Dutch types, particularly those of Van Dyck, which had hitherto dominated English printing. Apart from display types, for posters, handbills, mastheads and headlines, the types commonly used for books and newspapers were roman and italic in the following sizes: Pica (12 point), Small Pica (c.11pt), Long Primer (c.10pt), Brevier (c. 8pt), Nonpareil (c.6pt), and Pearl (c.5pt). Lee probably bought the associated leading, reglets, furniture and inks from London tradesmen, as the London printing trade, long-established, had spawned many ancillary suppliers.

Copperplate, or 'intaglio', printing of engraved illustrations and maps was done on a wooden-framed 'rolling press', rather like a large mangle, with wooden (later iron or steel) cylinders and a wooden bed. The turning motion was provided by a 'star-wheel', with four long wooden spokes for heaving around, winding the bed of the press between the cylinders. The engraved copper plate was covered with a stiff black ink, making sure that it was pressed well into the grooves formed by the engraver's burin. The excess ink was then wiped off, and a final burnish given to the surface of the plate, which was then placed on the bed of the press. The dampened paper being laid onto the inked plate, this was then covered with a woollen blanket and the bed and plate then rolled through between the cylinders, squeezing the paper well into the grooves, thus picking up the ink from even the finest of engraved lines. This process had to be repeated for each impression. Copperplate engraving and printing were trades in their own right, quite distinct from letterpress, although sometimes carried out under the same roof.

The paper used for book, newspaper, pamphlet and related letterpress printing was strong, light and made from cotton rags – old linen sheets and shirts, mixed with water and pulped, and formed into sheets by lifting a wood and wire-mesh frame up through the pulp to capture a thin layer on the mesh. The parallel wires of the mesh created a slightly ribbed appearance and feel to the paper, especially apparent when held up to the light; this is known as 'laid' paper. Cotton rag paper, being free of chemicals has the advantage of lasting for centuries, unlike the later wood-pulp paper. British paper-making had a long history – almost as long as its printing history (which dated from the 1470s) – with John Tate of Hertford producing paper used in a book printed in 1494, and John Spilman establishing a paper mill at Dartford in Kent by 1588. By 1786 the domestic paper industry was so large that seven-eighths of the paper used in Britain was made in England.

There had actually been a paper mill near Lewes, on the Ouse at Barcombe Bridge. This had been started by James Lopdell, draper of Lewes in, or before, 1702 and appears to have supplied the London market by sea, but this mill was demolished in 1716. The next paper mill in, or near, Lewes was that erected in the Pells in 1802, Arthur Lee having a hand in this. In 1809 another paper mill was erected at Isfield Lock. There was, therefore, no paper production locally in the time of William Lee and Paine.

Given that the north Kent coast had become a centre of paper-making, given the often poor state of the roads, and given the Lopdell precedent, it is possible that Lee's paper was carried by the coastwise trade – sailing barge, wherry or similar vessel – east along the Thames estuary, around the North Foreland, through The Downs past Deal, Dover and the Goodwins, west past Dungeness, Fairlight and Beachy, and finally up the Ouse. While it is possible that Lee's presses (easily dismantled and erected) and type came via this route, it is more probable that the regular carrier brought these.

Newspaper page sizes tended to increase as the century went on; a typical page in 1730 was 18 x 12 inches, while by 1757 it was 22 x 16½ inches. The Sussex Weekly Advertiser in 1789 was 18½ x 12½ inches, which probably had changed little, if at all, since 1746, but in 1790 it was increased to 19½ x 13 inches. Liable for the stamp tax, newspaper publishers bought large sheets of stamped paper and cut them in half to reduce the unit cost. Thus a 'double-demy' sheet (35 x 22½ inches) could be divided into two 'demy' sheets (22½ x 17½ inches), giving a page size of 17½ x 11¼ inches).

William Lee was, with Paine (who had moved to Lewes in 1768), a member of the White Hart Evening Club, a debating society. Coloured by Whiggery and republicanism, the *Journal* reprinted the letters of 'Junius,' attacking the government. Other articles criticised the British state and its colonial system, 'Tory tormenters,' English despotism, the nobility, the gulf between rich and poor, superstition (in the name of 'liberty of the mind,' 'plain truth' and 'common sense,') and praised public virtue. Lee was also an enthusiastic supporter of Wilkes (who had a private press at his house in London), whom he viewed as a 'great patriot.' In August 1770, Wilkes passed through Lewes, where he was given a hero's welcome with pealing bells and applauding crowds, and it is possible that Paine met him on this occasion. All raised the cry of 'Wilkes and Liberty,' evidence that Wilkes's appeal to the people and the 'rights of electors' met with popular support. By raising the question of rights, Wilkes had brought into the area of public debate the crucial issues of the basic rights of the people (i.e. the King's subjects), the relationship between the electorate (at that time only a tiny proportion of the population) and its representatives, and public influence on the structures of government and the constitution.

In 1772 Lee, who in that year moved his press to 64 High Street, on the south side (near the present Gorringe's premises), printed Tom Paine's famous first pamphlet, *The Case of the Officers of Excise* (4,000 copies, for distribution to the Excise Officer subscribers and potential sympathisers). Printing this pamphlet was hardly a challenge for the Lee family business. Its small format meant that thoughtful imposition (the arrangement of pages of type in the forme) could significantly reduce the number of pulls required. And of course the paper and printing were paid for by the subscribers.

William Lee's sons, William (1747-1830) and Arthur (1759-1824), joined him in the business, and the young William succeeded to it in 1786 on the death of his father, the firm becoming W. & A. Lee. Many other members of the extended Lee family were involved. William Lee I traded from 1745 to 1786 (the year of his death) as a printer, newspaper publisher, bookseller and stationer. Lee & Co (William Lee and his sons) traded as booksellers, stationers, bookbinders, newspaper proprietors, and letterpress and copperplate printers, circulating librarians and papermakers, from 1745 to 1839. William & Arthur Lee traded as printers from 1745 to 1801. M. (Margaret?) Lee was recorded as a printer in 1785.

Finis

Acknowledgements

Peter Chasseaud acknowledged Dr Colin Brent in his article about Lewes printing in the 18th Century, as do I for Colin's steadfast support throughout the years taken in this research.

Thanks to Melvyn Bragg for his encouragement.

Thanks to Jason Isbit for his editing and proof reading.

Thanks to Dr Michael Turner who was the first proof reader.

Thanks to Professor Richard Whatmore without whom I would never have embarked on this deeper research of Paine's time in Lewes.

Thanks to Dr Shane Horwell. We were together when he was an undergraduate in Intellectual History when we found the missing signatures. Shane was most helpful in organising the manuscripts of George Hindmarch at that time.

Thanks to my fellow committee members of The Thomas Paine Society UK, Professor Richard Whatmore (Chairman), David Ward (Secretary), Stuart Wright (Treasurer), Robert Morrell (Editor of the Journal) and Melvyn Bragg (President) for allowing me the freedom to write this book.